MASTERING
^THE UPSELL

Strategies for Increasing Revenue with Existing Clients.

@VICTORANTONIO
VICTORANTONIO.COM

More !

Antonio

D1379822

Published by Sellinger Group

Copyright © 2022 by Victor Antonio

Cover art by Camille Gonzalez

ISBN: 9798487318619

All Rights Reserved. No part of this publication may be produced in any form or by any means, mechanical or electronic, including photocopy and recording, or by any information storage and retrieval system, without the permission in writing from the author or publisher; exceptions are made for brief excerpts used in published reviews.

This publication is designed to provide accurate and authoritative information in regard to the subject matter covered. It is sold with the understanding that the publisher is not engaged in rendering legal, accounting, or other professional services. If legal advice or other expert assistance is required, the services of a competent professional should be sought.

This Sellinger Group Publication Edition is published by Victor Antonio of the Sellinger Group.

Contact Information:

PO Box 4342,

Alpharetta, GA 30023

www.SellingerGroup.com

Printed in the United States of America First Printing:

January, 2022

Library of Congress Cataloging in Publication Data

Antonio, Victor

Mastering The Upsell, Strategies for Increasing Revenue With Existing Clients

CONTENTS

PART 1: WHY UPSELLING

Chapter #1: Acres of Diamonds

Chapter #2: A Third Option

Chapter #3: CAC < CLV

Chapter #4: Propensity to Buy

Chapter #5: The Upselling Mindset

PART 2: HOW TO UPSELL

Upselling Strategy #1: Freemium to Premium

Upselling Strategy #2: Multiple Options

Upselling Strategy #3: Decoys

Upselling Strategy #4: Endowment

Upselling Strategy #5: Decision Fatigue

Upselling Strategy #6: Down-Sell to Upsell

Upselling Strategy #7: Below-At-Above

Upselling Strategy #8: In-Return Upsell

Upselling Strategy #9: The Eyes Have It

Upselling Strategy #10: Funnels and Ladders

Upselling Strategy #11: Reframing Value

Upselling Strategy #12: Utilization Rate

Upselling Strategy #13: Make it a Process

Upselling Strategy #14: Phrases + Why

Upselling Strategy #15: Mine Your Losses

Upselling Strategy #16: Compensate the Upsell

Appendix A: Outbound vs. Inbound

Appendix B: Discounting - The Easy Way Out

Appendix C: Client Conversation Model

CHAPTER 1

Acres of Diamonds

Before we jump deep into the subject matter of this book, I want to share a story that has impacted my thinking and modus operandi in business and, more specifically, selling. I beg you, the reader's indulgence, and patience as you read this story which was delivered more than 5,000 times by Russell Conwell during his lifetime.

When I first heard the story, I thought it was just like any other story, entertaining and interesting. But 3 decades have passed and I still find myself reflecting on the great lesson it has to offer. It is my hope that this story and the lessons embedded within will shift your business and sales perspective from scarcity to abundance, from helpless to hopeful, and from myopia to polyopia. Here is the story as told by Russell Conwell, entitled *Acres of Diamonds:*

When going down the Tigris and Euphrates rivers many years ago with a party of English travelers, I found myself under the direction of an old Arab guide whom we hired up at Baghdad. I have often thought how that guide resembled our barbers in certain mental characteristics. He thought that it was not only his duty to guide us down those rivers, and do what he was paid, but to also entertain us with stories curious and weird, ancient and modern, strange and familiar. Many of them I have forgotten, and I am glad I have, but there is one I shall never forget.

The old guide was leading my camel by its halter along the banks of those ancient rivers, and he told me story after story until I grew weary of his storytelling and ceased to listen.

I have never been irritated with that guide more than when he lost his temper as I ceased listening. But I remember that he took off his Turkish cap and swung it in a circle to get my attention. I could see it from the corner of my eye, but I determined not to look straight at him for fear he would tell another story.

I did finally look, and as soon as I did, he went right into another story.

Said he, "I will tell you a story now which I reserve for my particular friends." When he emphasized the words 'particular friends', I listened, and I have ever been glad I did. I am devoutly thankful that there are 1,674 young men who have been carried through college by this lecture who are also glad that I listened.

The old guide told me that there once lived not far from the River Indus an ancient Persian by the name of Ali Hafed.

He said that Ali Hafed owned a very large farm. That he had orchards, grain fields, and gardens. That he had money at interest and was a wealthy and contented man. One day there visited an ancient Buddhist priest, one of the wise men of the East. He sat down by the fire and told Ali Hafed how this old world of ours was made.

He said that this world was once a mere bank of fog, and that the Almighty thrust His finger into this bank of fog, and began slowly to move His finger around, increasing the speed until at last He whirled this bank of fog into a solid ball of fire. Then it

6

went rolling through the universe, burning its way through other banks of fog, and condensed the moisture without, until it fell in floods of rain upon its hot surface, and cooled the outward crust. Then, the internal fires bursting outward through the crust threw up the mountains and hills, the valleys, the plains and prairies of this wonderful world of ours. If this internal molten mass came bursting out and cooled very quickly, it became granite, less quickly copper, less quickly silver, less quickly gold, and, after gold, diamonds were made.

Said the old priest, "A diamond is a congealed drop of sunlight." (That is literally scientifically true.)

The old priest told Ali Hafed that if he had one diamond the size of his thumb he could purchase the country, and if he had a mine of diamonds, he could place his children upon thrones through the influence of their great wealth.

Ali Hafed had heard all about diamonds, how much they were worth, and he went to his bed that night a 'poor' man (emphasis added). He had not lost anything, but he was poor because he was discontented, and discontented because he feared he was poor.

He said to himself, "I want a mine of diamonds," and he lay awake all night. Early the next morning he sought out the priest. I know by experience that a priest is very cross when awakened early in the morning, and when he shook that old priest out of his dreams, Ali Hafed said to him,

"Will you tell me where I can find diamonds?"

"Diamonds! What do you want with diamonds?"

"Why, I wish to be immensely rich."

"Well then. Go and find them. That is all you have

7

to do. Go and find them, and then you will have them."

"But I don't know where to go."

"You will find a river that runs through white sands, between high mountains. In those white sands you will always find diamonds."

"I don't believe there is any such river.""Oh yes, there are plenty of them. All you have to do is go and find them. And then you will have diamonds."

Said Ali Hafed, "I will go."

He sold his farm, collected his money, left his family in the charge of a neighbor, and away he went in search of diamonds. He began his search, very properly to my mind, at the Mountains of the Moon. Afterward he came around into Palestine, then wandered on into Europe, and at last when his money was all spent and he was in rags, wretchedness, and poverty, he stood on the shore of that bay at Barcelona, in Spain, when a great tidal wave came rolling in between the pillars of Hercules, and the poor, afflicted, suffering, dying man could not resist the awful temptation to cast himself into that incoming tide, and he sank beneath its foaming crest, never to rise in this life again.

After that old guide had told me that awfully sad story, he stopped the camel I was riding and went back to fix the baggage that was coming off another camel, and I had an opportunity to muse over his story while he was gone. I remember saying to myself,

"Why did he reserve that story for his 'particular friends'?" There seemed to be no beginning, no middle, no end, nothing to it."

That was the first story I had ever heard told in my life,

8

and would be the first one I ever read, in which the hero was killed in the first chapter. I had but one chapter of that story, and the hero was dead.

When the guide came back and took up the halter of my camel, he went right ahead with the story, into the second chapter, just as though there had been no break.

The man who purchased Ali Hafed's farm one day led his camel into the garden to drink, and as that camel put its nose into the shallow water of the garden brook, Ali Hafed's successor noticed a curious flash of light from the white sands of the stream. He pulled out a black stone that had an eye of light reflecting all the hues of the rainbow. He took the pebble into the house and put it on the mantel which covered the central fire, and forgot all about it.

A few days later this same old priest came in to visit Ali Hafed's successor, and the moment he opened the drawing-room door he saw a flash of light on the mantel. He rushed up to it, and shouted,

"Here is a diamond! Has Ali Hafed returned?"

"Oh no, Ali Hafed has not returned, and that is not a diamond. That is nothing but a stone we found right here in our own garden."

"But," said the priest, "I tell you I know a diamond when I see it. I know that this is a diamond."

Together they rushed out into the old garden and stirred up the white sands with their fingers, and lo! There came up more beautiful and valuable gems than the first.

"Thus," said the guide to me, "was discovered the diamond mine of Golconda, the most magnificent diamond mine in all the history of mankind, excelling the Kimberly itself. The Kohinoor and the Orloff of the crown jewels of England and Russia, the largest on earth, came from that mine."

After the old Arab guide finished telling me the second chapter of his story, he took off his Turkish cap and swung it around in the air, to draw my attention to the moral of the story. Those Arab guides have morals to their stories, although they are not always moral.

As he swung his hat, he said to me, "Had Ali Hafed remained at home and dug in his own cellar, or underneath his own wheat fields, or in his own garden, instead of wretchedness, starvation, and death by suicide in a strange land, he would have had 'acres of diamonds'. For every acre of that old farm, yes, every shovelful, afterward revealed gems that have since decorated the crowns of monarchs."

The value of this story will become apparent, if it already hasn't, in the subsequent chapters. The diamonds we seek are opportunities. There are acres of opportunities all around us. All we have to do is see them. No matter what company you work for, salespeople are told that if they do these five things, they will be successful:

1) **Product:** Know your product better than your clients so you can position your self as an authority.

2) **Present:** Be able to articulate the product (or service) value during a presentation. That's how you outsell your competition, by positioning its value.

3) **Process:** In order to sell consistently, you have to have an effective sales process.

4) **Prospect:** Your ability to find new clients will determine your level of success. Keep your sales pipeline filled with potential clients.

5) Persuade: Knowing how to ask for a commitment is: what to say, how to say and when to say it will allow you to close more deals.

This is rock solid advice especially if you're just starting out with a company or just starting your business. Your ability to generate revenue is directly proportional to your ability to acquire new clients.

Here's the sales sequence for success:

Product - Present - Prospect - Process - Persuade

And, after a deal is closed (i.e. the client has been persuaded to buy), many then jump right back to prospecting for new leads provided by marketing, or asking existing clients for referrals.

Unfortunately, many companies don't have a formal process for asking for referrals and, opportunities are lost. The pushback from salespeople range from not feeling comfortable asking for referrals or simply not having the time to follow up on referrals. My guess is that

(A) they don't really understand the value of getting existing satisfied clients to give them a lead that is more likely to convert than a cold one,

(B) they don't understand how it shortens their sales cycle since they've never calculated the value of getting a referral, and

(C) no one has ever taught them a process or, it isn't part of their initial training.

Whatever the case, getting a referral beats prospecting for new leads. It's like getting handed a client who is more likely to say yes than no. What could be better than that?

What about a client who has already said "Yes"?

CHAPTER 2

A Third Option

It's fair to say that companies today find themselves, as they always have, focused on how to achieve higher profitability by either finding new ways to cut cost (increase operational efficiencies), expand their market share (increase customer base), generate more sales (increase revenues), or all the above.

The goal is always to beat last year's numbers, especially in the area of sales. Each year that number goes up. Revenue (sales) expectation is a variable that unfortunately doesn't conform to the law of gravity. What goes up must continue to go up.

Shareholders are riddled with value anxiety and it reveals itself through their impatience as they demand results, not excuses from their holdings. Regardless of market conditions or economic indicators, their expectations are tethered to what was forecasted, and what was promised. Warnings of potential market stagnation or, worse, contraction is but a footnote in their shareholder meeting notes.

Top executives feeling the acute pressure from shareholders then turn around and apply downward pressure on their directors and managers, demanding they find ways to cut costs but, more importantly, grow revenues from each of their business units.

12

Managers feeling the pressure from top executives then turn around and transfer that pressure to their salespeople, by pushing and driving them harder to find new clients, fill pipelines, increase their online conversions, or close rates offline.

From the salesperson's perspective, they're doing everything they can to bring in new business. They're hitting the phones, blasting out emails, and attempting to connect with potential clients on social media, all with the hope of generating interest and initiate a series of meetings to get new opportunities into the pipeline.

And therein lies the real challenge; getting a meeting. Let me state the obvious. Getting your foot in the door with an influencer or decision maker is harder than it has ever been. It's not difficult finding potential clients (i.e., prospects that fit your ideal client profile), the challenge is access to those potential clients.

OPTION #1: OUTBOUND

Outbound is a sales strategy whereby you reach 'out' to potential clients whether by email, social media channel, or the good old-fashioned way, by phone. Let's look at cold calling by phone, which has recently begun to make a comeback after being pronounced dead by social media pundits.

Cold calling a potential client today and connecting has become extremely difficult. Let's begin by looking at the numbers and how to calculate its efficiency.

A cold calling or Outbound campaign typically has key metrics (ratios) to measure its effectiveness: Call-to-Connect, Connect-to-Meeting, and Meeting-to-Close. (e.g., marketing lead versus a recommendation or referral).

Call-to-Connect (CTC) ratio is the number of times you were able to connect with the intended person within a company. For example, if you made 100 calls and you were able to get through to the intended person, that is considered a connection. A CTC ratio falls somewhere in the 3% to 8% range. Which means that out of 100 calls, you'll connect with the intended person 3 to 8 times (i.e., CTC ratio equals 3:100 or 8:100). CTC ratios will vary depending on your industry, number of competitors and other market factors. CTC ratios are also highly dependent on the source of the lead (e.g., marketing lead versus a recommendation or referral).

Connect-to-Meeting (CTM) ratio is the ability to convert that phone conversation (or online connection) into a face-to-face meeting with the contact. Once you connect with someone who fits your client profile and your sales pitch is persuasively tailored to pique their interest, then the chances of getting a face-to-face meeting or scheduling an online demonstration are high. A good rule-of-thumb for this ratio is 1 out of 3 or 33%.

Meeting-to-Close (MTC) ratio is the number of prospects you were able to convert to clients after a series of meetings or demonstrations. A good rule-of-thumb here is 1 out of 2 or 50%.

So, let's pull this all together. If you made 100 calls, you could expect to connect with up to 8 people (CTC = 3% to 8%). Let's be cautiously optimistic here and assume the salesperson was able to connect with 5 prospects. From those 5, you can expect to get 2 prospects (CTM = 40%) to agree to a face-to-face meeting or an online demo. Of those two, the salesperson is able to convert 1 into a client (MTC = 50%). Out of 100 clients, the salesperson was able to sell one deal. Let's call this the Call-To-Sale ratio, in this case 1:100[1].

1. The ratios vary by industry, but I like to use the 5% - 30% - 50% rule as a baseline or starting point. CTC = 5%, CTM = 30% and MTC = 50%.

Now, you can argue that a well-managed sales campaign should be able to produce better results than this, and you might be correct. Speculation aside, the big takeaway from this sketch analysis is the high volume of calls (or social connections) required to obtain a meeting and the depressingly low Call-to-Sales rate.

What isn't speculation is that once a salesperson is able to gain access to a decision-maker the chances for closing the deal jumps dramatically.

GAINING ACCESS

The biggest challenge salespeople face today is not finding potential clients or communicating values, but rather in gaining access to the right person(s) to make the buying decision. This is important. Most companies don't have a sales problem, they have an access problem.

Companies invest an inordinate amount of time, money and effort into improving a salesperson's product knowledge and selling skills. But in reality, the High-Leverage Activity (HLA) should be aimed at figuring out ways to get in front of the right people.

So, companies have doubled down and are shifting their efforts towards gaining access by investing in a variety of sales enablement tools (i.e., technology stack) for prospecting and tracking potential leads. At the center of this technological eco-system is a Customer Relationship Management (CRM) system which, if used properly, is able to track a lead through the full sales cycle or the client's buying process.

The latest sales mantra is, "If I can meet 'em, I can close 'em." Many salespeople brag that their MTC ratio is as high as 8:10, or 80%. There is little doubt that if they can get access and face-time with a prospect, they will greatly improve their chances of closing the deal. But we're still left with the horrendous Call-to-Sale (CTS) of 1:100. You can't close 'em if you can't meet 'em!

One variable I haven't touched on is the sales cycle; how long it takes to close a sale from first contact to close or from first call to close. Ask 10 companies what their sales cycle is, and you'll get 10 distinct answers. Ask them at different times of the year and you'll get another set of answers. Sales cycles are hard to predict because humans are unpredictable. Why? As the number of stakeholders (i.e., people with a vested interest in any change) involved in making a final decision, continues to grow, so too does the chance of conflict and cross interests that invariably leads to a no decision or delayed decision.

I hesitate to put a number on how many stakeholders are involved in a buying decision, especially in B2B (Business-to-Business) sales, since each company and scenario will vary. Some studies put the number at 5 stakeholders involved in a decision while others put it as high as 9. Whatever the number, with each additional stakeholder added to the buying process, the sales cycle gets extended, thereby adding to the Cost of Sale (COS) and management's frustration with salespeople.

Managers instruct salespeople to do "whatever it takes" to get in front of qualified prospects and close more deals. That's easier said than done with so many personalities, all with competing agendas, involved in a buying decision.

It's no wonder only 53% of salespeople achieve or exceed their revenue goal, according to CSO insights, who every year release a study on sales performance. That number has been in steady decline for the last 5 years and continues to trend downward slowly[2] .

Bottomline? Outbound is hard, it's not getting easier and the cost of acquiring a new client continues to go up.

OPTION #2: INBOUND

With the realities of Outbound being what they are, many companies have shifted their marketing and advertising dollars from Outbound campaigns to Inbound or pull marketing strategies. Inbound simply means that the prospect discovers you and calls you. The lure of Inbound, the siren song if you will, is to escape the harsh reality of cold calling mentioned in the previous section.

Many books have been written about the demise of cold calling corresponding with the rise of the Internet, more specifically social media. Studies have been published on how customers are now well-informed and, therefore, more reluctant to take a cold call, let alone agree to a meeting.

It's an established fact that buyers review many sources of information before contacting a vendor or supplier and, when they do, their buying preferences have almost been formed. The bad news? Clients are more informed, more demanding, know what they want, and they have options (i.e., other vendors willing to give them a better deal).

The good news is that your company is receiving calls from prospects who have prequalified themselves by making the call. Think about it: Prospects first go online to research options in search of the right product or service with the right benefits. When a prospect calls a company, it's usually because they haven't been able to resolve some lingering doubt or seek more clarification from the information gleaned from your

2. The Growing Buyer-Seller Gap - Results of the 2018 Buyer Preferences Study, CSO Insights

company's website, case studies, blogs, videos, etc.

Therefore, when a prospect makes the effort to call your company, it's usually because they are almost convinced, being well into the buying process, that your company has the product or service they desire. In contacting you, they have, in essence, qualified themselves as an ideal or strong potential buyer.

This is where marketing plays a pivotal role. Prospects go online to research a product, which means they want to consume quality content, they want to be educated. Marketing used to be about sizzle, branding, colors, designs, layout, catchy phrases, etc. Today, marketing has evolved into a dual role: grab a prospect's attention, and help prospects form a preference for their product.

Grabbing a prospect's attention in today's market is tough given all of the marketing noise, competitive clutter, and differentiating distractions on the Internet today.

Marketing departments have been forced to level-up their creativity by developing more sophisticated and comprehensive product launch campaigns. Beyond the cool graphics and slick animations, they must also seek to educate the customer using a variety of channels and collaterals: white papers, case studies, videos, blogs, podcasts, product placement, sponsorships, billboards, and so on.

It's no wonder marketing expenses have increased gradually. Marketing budgets typically average about 10% of a company's total budget or about 5% of a company's revenue, with obvious variation from one industry to another.

The siren song of Inbound marketing is strong. Companies claim that Inbound marketing strategies produce a better Return on Investment (ROI) and generate a better lead (sales) Conversion

Rates (CR) than Outbound. Depending on which study you choose to believe, the conversion rate of a lead generated from a company's website is somewhere around 5%.

From a high-level vantage point the preferred strategy between Inbound and Outbound seems to be a foregone conclusion. A 5% conversion rate (5:100) is a whole lot better than 1% (1:100). Add to this a lower cost per lead (i.e., lower COS), and it's no wonder that marketing dollars have increased and have been shifted from Outbound efforts to Inbound efforts.

So, does Inbound have any shortcomings? Of course it does.

First, you can't control the quality of prospects who call in, which means customer support has more calls to sift through to find real buyers. The customer support department may not be part of the marketing budget, which then hides the true cost of any marketing campaign.

Second, prospects who found your company online may (a) not buy as much (i.e., revenue spend per customer) or, worse, (b) only buy from you because of some special offer (i.e., price). This type of customer would be considered a low-quality buyer who isn't loyal and will leap to the next supplier if the opportunity (i.e., better price, new technology, enhanced service) presents itself.

Third, these types of buyers also have the tendency to use up more of your company's support resources and can often be quite demanding and vocal, which in turn, may negatively impact your Customer Satisfaction (CSAT) metric or Net Promoter Score (NPS).

And lastly, companies have no control over how many people discover them. Unlike a cold calling campaign where you're reaching out to targeted prospects, with Inbound, you get what you get. There is no quality control. So, while many may pre-qualify themselves by contacting you, that doesn't necessarily mean that they're quality clients. With Outbound, your problem is access to decision-makers. With Inbound, your problem is quantity (the number of prospects you're able to attract) and quality (ideal prospect that fits your targeted profile).

In the real world, there are no binary solutions (i.e., one or the other), Inbound or Outbound. Which is why companies today employ a mix of the two, combining Inbound marketing efforts with sales Outbound playbooks.

But, can there be a third option? An option that insures both quantity and quality? Much like the Acres of Diamonds story, there are opportunities right in our own data-ladened backyard.

OPTION #3: UPSELLING

Whether you're employing an Inbound or Outbound marketing strategy or both, the reality is that the cost of acquiring a new client continues to grow at a nonlinear rate. The goal of any viable company is to reduce Customer Acquisition Costs (CAC) while at the same time increasing a Customer's Lifetime Value (CLV).

Let's define the two:

Customer Acquisition Cost (CAC) is the total cost associated with all activities, usually marketing and sales, in acquiring a new client. This could include things like: content creation, ad spend, employee salaries, travel, meeting preparation, proposal development, and so on.

Client Lifetime Value (CLV) is how much a loyal client will buy from you over a given period of time. A good average is

3 years.

One could argue that Outbound marketing is better at increasing CLV but falls short of reducing CAC. That's because with Outbound, you can control the types of clients you go after, but the sales cycle to connect and close those clients will be longer and will thereby increase your CAC.

On the other hand, Inbound marketing does a great job at reducing CAC but fails to find the type of clients to increase CLV (i.e., you may attract clients who are only looking for a good deal and won't be loyal).

Much like the farmer who was looking for diamonds in far off lands, both Inbound and Outbound strategies are focused on what new segments or opportunities lie ahead in some distant market. Meanwhile, right beneath their feet is a strategy that can reduce their CAC and increase their CLV at the same time. A strategy that has been altogether ignored. I'll repeat that; *altogether ignored!* A strategy that will guarantee the lowest possible CAC and increase the CLV by extending customer loyalty and increasing their spend with the company. That strategy, which has fallen between the cracks of Inbound and Outbound, is Upselling!

Now, let's take a moment to define Upselling and how the term will be used throughout the book.

According to Wikipedia, "Upselling is the practice in which a business tries to persuade customers to purchase a higher-end product, an upgrade, or an additional item in order to make a more profitable sale. For instance, a salesperson may influence a customer into purchasing the newest version of an item, rather than the less expensive current model, by pointing out its additional features [3]."

3. http://www.wikipedia.org

21

Anyone who's bought an expensive piece of electronic equipment has most likely experienced an internal (you on you) or external (others on you) Upsell.

An internal upsell is where you talk yourself into buying a more expensive option when you compare the features and benefits against the price difference. The mere exposure to something better might influence your decision to consider buying it. For example, if you're looking to buy a large screen television, you might have your heart set on a 52-inch certain screen size. Next to that television in a 60-inch version for only $150 more.

Immediately, your mind races as to whether it's worth spending a little more to get a better screen size. Your internal dialogue might go something like this:

"Hmm. For only $150 more I can get a bigger screen. It might be better for watching action films. I mean, my last television lasted 5 years so maybe I should get it. What's an extra $150 spread over five years? Yeah, I think I'll go with the big one or else I'll regret it."

Does any of that sound familiar? Whether you're exposed to a better option or it's merely mentioned by a third party, your brain can't help but initiate a cost-benefit analysis.

An external Upsell is when you are presented with a more expensive and valuable option by a third party. For example, a salesperson noticing you looking at various televisions walks over and suggests that a bigger screen size might be a better bang for your buck. The salesperson gives you their opinion on why it's a better deal, provides valuable insight, and you decide to go with the bigger screen.

I should note that an external upsell isn't always presented by a salesperson. Sometimes it's an option presented to you by an application on a website. If you've purchased something from Amazon online in the past, then I'm sure you're familiar with their comparative matrix where they show you other similar products, usually a bit richer in feature and price. The use of this matrix is meant to influence your decision-making process. More on this later in the book.

Now let's look at Cross-Selling. Upselling is focused mainly on enhancing the sale. Cross-selling focuses on offering the customer something completely apart from the item under consideration that may or may not complement it.

For example, if you go to McDonalds and order a combo meal (burger, fries and a soft drink), you may be asked,

"Do you want to supersize your order?"

Which means, "Do you want a combo meal with more fries and a larger drink?"

The price differential might be, let's say, $1. Your brain does an immediate gut check and you decide to supersize the order. That's a perfect example of an Upsell. The original item under consideration (i.e., combo meal) was enhanced. Much like the 52-inch television example. For only $150 more, you can have the 60-inch version.

In a Cross-Sell, you are buying something in addition to the item under consideration, which may or may not complement it. For instance, the salesperson at the electronic store will suggest you buy additional accessories (e.g., wall mount, specific cables, surge protector) to ensure a better viewing experience with your television. If you're buying a computer, the salesperson might suggest a software application and some in-store training courses for that particular software. When you get to the checkout counter, the person there might ask if you would like to buy an additional 1-year warranty for your new television. These are all examples of Cross-Selling.

The easiest way to remember if it's a Cross-Sell or an Upsell is to think of going to get a burger at McDonalds. If you order a burger and the cashier asks, "Would you like to supersize (i.e., bigger burger) your order?", that's an Upsell. If the cashier asks, "Would you like fries with that burger?", that's a Cross-Sell.

If you're on Amazon and the recommendation engine suggests enhanced options (e.g., bigger screen size) for the item under consideration, that's an Upsell. If the recommendation engine shows you 'people who bought this also bought this' these other complementary items, that's a Cross-Sell.

I realize that the examples I've given are Business-to-Consumer (B2C) type of transactions, but the same holds true in a Business-to-Business (B2B) environment.

For example, if your company sells capacity or bandwidth at a data center, you can offer the client different levels of service depending on their needs. One client may want to buy X speed and Y storage capacity at price #1. You can Upsell them on higher speed or capacity and even Cross-Sell them on a Service Level Agreement (SLA) that guarantees minimal downtime.

Throughout the book I will continue to use the word Upsell to represent both Upselling and Cross-Selling. And every strategy in this book can be applied to both B2C and B2B scenarios. You're only limited by your own creativity when it comes to applying the strategies that we're about to cover.

The way forward to new and insured revenues is exploiting, in the value-centric sense, your existing client base. Upselling conversion rates are far higher than both Inbound and Outbound combined, yet few companies have a documented or formalized process for doing so. It's time to explore, understand and begin mining the acres of revenue opportunities all around you.

According to Marketing Metrics[4], the probability of converting an existing customer is 60% to 70%. The probability of converting a new prospect, on the other hand, is only 5% to 20%. Simply put, Upselling speeds up your time to higher profitability by reducing your Client Acquisition Cost (CAC) and shortening your sales cycle, thereby reducing overall Cost of Sales (COS) but also by increasing your Customer's Lifetime Value (CLV). Let's dig into this more in the next chapter.

4. http://www.marketingmetrics.com

CHAPTER 3

CAC < CLV

"We showed that in industry after industry, the high cost of acquiring customers renders many customer relationships unprofitable during their early years. Only in later years, when the cost of serving loyal customers falls and the volume of their purchases rises, do relationships generate big returns. The bottom line: increasing customer retention rates by 5% increases profits by 25% to 95%." - *Frederick F. Reichheld and Phil Schefter of the Harvard Business School*

I'm a fan of the television series Shark Tank (or Dragon's Den if you're in the UK), where entrepreneurs present their product ideas to a panel of investors, also known as sharks, hoping to get funding in exchange for a percentage of their company.

One of the sharks is Kevin O'Leary, whose brash, no-holds-barred, in-your-face, truth-telling often leaves entrepreneurs stammering and stuttering as they come under the barrage of his tough questions.

In an interview, O'Leary stated that one of the first things he looks for when determining whether to invest in a company or not is their Customer Acquisition Cost (CAC) and the Lifetime Value (LTV) of a customer. In his mind the math is simple; if your CAC is less than your LTV, you have a business. If the opposite is true, you're in trouble and he won't invest.

CAC < LTV

O'Leary is correct in identifying the CAC as a true north metric when it comes to business growth and sustainability. Many companies engage in casting a wide marketing net to try to capture new clients. The problem with this approach is that the wider the cast, the more money you'll spend and the quality of the catch, clients, are unknown.

Like in all marketing efforts, you need to consider three variables when it comes to spending money on advertisement:

- Where you cast (online, offline or both)

- How you cast (types of advertisements)

- What you're casting for (target audience)

Given that you can't market to everyone, since that would be cost-prohibitive and wasteful, companies are becoming acutely aware that target marketing for the right customers (i.e., loyal customer types) is a long-term winning strategy. The key ques-tion then becomes, "How do you get quality clients while keeping your sales and marketing cost down?"

The first step is to determine how to calculate your Client Acquisition Cost (CAC). The easiest way to calculate your CAC is by adding up all the costs associated with both sales and marketing efforts and dividing that number by the number of new customers acquired during a given time period or marketing campaign.

$$CAC = \frac{\text{Total Cost of Sales and Marketing}}{\text{Number of Customers Acquired}}$$

Here's a simple example. Your company decides to participate in an upcoming event, a trade show, where it will cost $3,000 to register and another $7,000 for the booth space where you can set up a display to promote your company along with a free quarter-page ad in the event guide. Up to this point, the total cost is $10,000, which hits the marketing budget. Now, you'll have to have people in the booth, let's say 2, to answer customer questions and qualify new leads. The cost of these 2 people would include their daily salary cost, travel expenses, hotel, per diem, and other expenses. For the sake of this example, let's say it will cost the company $5,000 in total to have 2 people in the booth for 2 days and allow for 2 days of travel to and from the event. Total marketing and sales cost is $15,000 ($10,000 plus $5,000).

Now, during those 2 days, 100 leads were collected. Upon returning to the home office after the event, the 2 salespeople begin to make follow-up phone calls to qualify each lead with the intent of setting up a meeting, which in turn would lead to a proposal and an eventual deal. For the sake of simplicity, let's say that after qualifying the 100 opportunities over the phone, only 10 were legitimately interested in the product or device. After meeting with each of the 10 companies, doing a demonstration and submitting a proposal, 5 companies decided to buy.

It's worth noting that qualifying clients over the phone, doing on-site demonstrations and preparing proposals are additional costs that should be added to the numerator (total Cost of Sales and marketing). Let's keep the calculation simple by assuming it's already incorporated or accounted for into the total cost (i.e., $15,000).

Next, you calculate the CAC by simply taking the total Cost of Sales and marketing ($15,000) for this event and dividing it by the number of prospects (leads) who actually purchased (5) your product or service. That means that each lead was worth $3,000 ($15,000 divided by 5), or said another way, the cost of acquiring a new client was $3,000.

Another example would be if you ran an online advertising campaign that costs your company $5,000 for a month. At the end of the month you conclude, based on your tracking data, that the number of clients who viewed the ad and bought from you is 10. Your CAC would be $500 ($5,000 divided by 10).

Now that you have the cost of acquiring a new client, the next step is to determine the value of these clients based on how long they intend to continue buying from you. In other words, how much will they buy from you over a given period? This question has two variables to consider: how much, and how long.

When we talk about Customer Lifetime Value, it's important to establish what timeframe you want to set as 'lifetime'. For example, a hardware store like Lowes or Home Depot may have a time-frame of 10 years, whereas a Starbucks coffee shop might have its lifetime number set at 20 years.

STARBUCKS CALCULATIONS

Starbucks is a well-recognized brand that has expanded globally and has taken a lot of my money as I visit them frequently. Neil Patel, Chief Marketing Officer at NPDigital, gives a great example of how Starbucks analyzes the value of each customer [5].

Customer Lifetime Value (CLV) is the total amount of revenue derived from a customer over a given period (i.e., their lifetime buying from your company).

5. https://neilpatel.com/blog/customer-acquisition-cost/

Step 1: The Numbers

(S) is the customer expenditure per visit:

Customer 1: $3.90

Customer 2: $8.50

Customer 3: $5.00

Customer 4: $6.50

Customer 5: $6.00

Average across 5 customers = $5.90

(C) is the number of visits per week (purchase cycle):

Customer 1: 4

Customer 2: 3

Customer 3: 5

Customer 4: 6

Customer 5: 3

Average across 5 customers = 4.20

(A) is the average spend per week:

Customer 1: $14.00

Customer 2: $25.50

Customer 3: $25.00

Customer 4: $39.00

Customer 5: $18.00

Average spend across 5 customers = $24.30

(T) is the average customer lifespan (how long someone remains a client or customer) in the case of Starbucks in 20 years.

(P) equals profit margin per customer is 21.3%

Step 2: Two Ways to Calculate CLV

Option #1: Simple CLV

1 Year = 52 weeks

(A) Average spend per week: $24.30

(T) Average customer lifespan: 20 years

$$\text{CLV} = 52 \times (A) \times (T)$$

$$52 \times \$24.30 \times 20 \text{ years} = \$25{,}272$$

Option #2: Average CLV gross margin per Customer lifespan equation

(T) Average customer lifespan: 20 years

(S) Customer expenditure per visit: $5.90

(C) Number of visits per week: 4.20

(P) Profit margin per customer: 21.3%

Average CLV Gross Margin $= (T)(52 \times S \times C \times P)$

$$20 \times (52 \times \$5.90 \times \$4.2 \times .213) = \$5{,}489.94$$

We should keep in mind that both of these CLV numbers are over a 20-year lifespan. Many companies, in fact the majority of companies, won't be around in 20 years, so these calculations might seem a bit fanciful for the average small to medium-sized company and startups.

That said, a shorter time frame should be used to calculate your CLV. It might be worth researching your market and finding out the average lifespan of a client and run your own numbers.

The main point here is that calculating your CLV will give you an idea of how much money you need to invest in acquiring new clients. While this might be difficult for startups who have no purchase history to rely upon, using shorter timeframes (e.g., 3 years) provides a baseline from which to calculate your initial CLV.

Lifetime value and what is lifetime are hard numbers to calculate, especially if you don't have any historical data. If you don't have reliable data, a good rule-of-thumb is to use the 3-30 rule. The average lifetime value of a client is 3 years, and during those 3 years they'll buy 30% more of the original purchase from your company.

Let's go back to the trade show example where the CAC is $3,000 and determine if the tradeshow was a good marketing investment. Assume that after adding up the total sales from those five clients we arrive at a revenue number of $50,000. That means that the average client purchased $10,000 ($50,000 divided by 5 clients) worth of products or services or both.

If this were the case, then the Return on Investment (ROI) is calculated by:

ROI = (($10,000 - $3,000)/ $3,000) *100 = **233%**.

Not bad!

$$ROI = \frac{(Sales - Investment)}{Investment} \times 100$$

Now, if instead of $10,000 in sales per new client the number was $3,000, would the investment (i.e., ROI of 0%) in the Now, if instead of $10,000 in sales per new client the number was $3,000, would the investment (i.e., ROI of 0%) in the trade show still be worth the effort of acquiring a new client? The answer is it depends. It depends on your value horizon, short-term or long-term.

If a company is starved for revenues and is looking for immediate short-term ROI, then the trade show would be considered a bust and not worth doing again at zero percent ROI.

But what if the company was playing a long-term or infinite game where an acquired client today meant future revenue over a specified timeframe (lifetime)? What if the company knew, based on historical data, that clients will buy, on average, an additional $5,000 after the first purchase ($3,000) over a 3-year timeframe (lifetime)? While the immediate ROI would be zero year one, the CAC < LTV formula holds ($3,000 < $8,000) over the 3-year period.

In this example, an ROI analysis could be used to get a snap-shot of your investment, whereas calculating the CAC and LVT relationship is a long-term view of the value each client will bring your company over a given period.

In the end, you need to collect data to really understand who your customers are, how much are they buying, what are they buying, and for how long are they buying. We can then use this data to reduce our Client Acquisition Costs by sharpening our marketing approach and targeting ideal clients who are more likely to buy, more likely to buy more, and more likely to stay on as loyal customers.

In the next chapter, let's take a look at what highly structured and organized companies are doing with the data they're collecting on customers and how technologies like Artificial Intelligence are being applied to extract meaningful insights like propensity to buy and propensity to buy more (i.e., Up-selling).

CHAPTER 4

Propensity To Buy

The power and use of artificial intelligence in business can take many forms, depending on what a company is attempting to achieve. In sales, the ability to predict 'who will' and 'who won't' is the single most powerful analytic tool a company can possess.

- Who will buy and who won't
- Who will cancel and who won't
- Who will renew and who won't

Unfortunately, predicting with certainty what a human being will do at a given time, when presented with a given option at a given price, is impossible.

Prediction is all about probability or something close (e.g., 'likelihood' or 'confidence' that some given thing will happen). Machine Learning is about taking Big Data as input and building a Predictive Model that might be used to 'score' the likelihood of something happening.

A Predictive Model generated from Machine Learning isn't an accurate science, but it's a great 'guesstimator' as to who is 'most likely' to make a favorable decision.

- Who will (most likely) buy and who won't

- Who will (most likely) cancel and who won't

- Who will (most likely) renew and who won't

In order to understand how Big Data, Machine Learning, and Predictive Models fit together, let's take a real world example. First, let's zoom out once more and understand the basic components:

- **Data:** This is the information that is to be analyzed. Now, this information can come from different sources, but let's assume that we'll use a particular company's database to analyze the last 5 years of data. The number of variables and the time period it encompasses are often referred to as the dataset. This is the INPUT.

- **Machine Learning:** This is a sophisticated algorithm developed by data scientists to analyze the data-set (input) with the objective of finding patterns about 'who will and who won't'.

- **Predictive Model:** This is another algorithm that extrapolates (predicts) based on patterns detected by the Machine Learning component. Previously, this would have been a simple linear-regression or time-series model of a type you might find in an Excel spreadsheet. However, the mathematics are far more sophisticated and have also been combined with a rule-based Artificial Intelligence (AI) component, the sum total of which is far more effective in determin-ing with high probability of success 'who will and who won't'. This is the **OUTPUT**.

Let's look at a common problem most companies have when trying to boost their revenues. Say you have a database of 50,000 potential clients (contacts). The dataset contains demographic information such as name, address, gender, marital status,

36

age, and geographic location, and behavioral information such as visits to the website, page views, download requests, demo requests, newsletter signups, and search terms that have been used.

Marketing has decided to do a mail-out to this list that will hopefully prompt the contacts to go to the website and purchase a new product (price = $500). Marketing estimates, based on past campaigns of this nature, indicate a response rate of 5%, which is deemed sufficient to justify the endeavor. Marketing then creates the flyer, uploads the contact database, presses the mail button, and sits back and waits for the results.

After a month, the results are in, and the numbers look like this:

Cost

Cost of mailer ($2 per)

x

Number of contacts (50,000)

= Total cost of $100,000

Even though we've mailed out to 50,000 potential buyers, not all of them are actually going to buy. Marketing therefore has to guess what percentage will respond to the marketing effort, and this guessing drives the C-Suite nuts! It's hard to predict 'who will and who won't'.

This scenario reminds me of John Wanamaker, an advertising pioneer who was quoted as saying, "Half the money I spend on advertising is wasted; the trouble is, I don't know which half."

My modern version would be, "Marketing is part science and part hope; the problem is, I don't know which to depend on."

A 3% response rate (i.e., the percentage of people who received the flyer, went to the website, and purchased the $500 item) would mean that 1,500 people bought.

Revenue

1,500 People who responded

x

$500 item price

= **Total Revenue of $750,000**

In this world, our 'sales' world, the bottom line is the only line that matters. If we calculate the profit by taking our total revenue and subtracting the total cost, we get:

Profit

$750,000 – $100,000

Total Profit = $650,000

Based on these results, the marketing campaign is judged as a success by the company, and everyone is happy. Marketing breathes a sigh of relief because, although their response rate was estimated at 5%, 3% still represents a win. Any rational business leader, after viewing this successful campaign, will ask four basic questions:

1. Can we do it again?
2. Will it be just as successful?
3. Can we improve the results?
4. If so, by how much?

Marketing will respond to the first question with a vigorous "yes we can". (After all, they'd like to remain relevant and keep their jobs.)

To the second question, "Will it be as successful?", they may feel good about what they've already done and respond in the affirmative.

To the third question, they may offer up ideas like, "If we improve the layout of the flyer, change the colors or fonts, and time the mail-out, we may be able to improve the results."

To the final question, they may have to make a 'finger-in-the-wind' guess, since their 5% prediction was off by 2% — quite a sizeable error.

This is how marketing has always operated: a series of campaigns with some successes and some failures, of course with hopefully more of the former and fewer of the latter. The key point is this all-too-typical marketing methodology is error-laden and inherently unpredictable.

It's now time for marketing to turn to Machine Learning to help improve the success rate and predictability of marketing campaigns.

Let's assume that Marketing take their customer data set, along with historical results of their various marketing campaigns, and feed that information (**INPUT**) into their Machine Learning Platform, which will produce a Predictive Model on 'who will and who won't' (**OUTPUT**).

Marketing now takes their list of 50,000 potential clients and runs it through their Predictive Model. The model then spits out a list of ONLY 3,000 who are 'more likely to buy'.

Cost

3,000 x $2/mailer = **$6,000**

Revenue

3,000 x $500 Item Price = **$1,500,000**

Profit

$1,500,000 – $6,000 = **$1,494,000**

Let's pause for a moment and analyze the profitability of this campaign.

These numbers show 100% of the contacts buying. This isn't reality. The model is giving us a select group of clients, based on the data set, who are 'more likely to buy than not'. This means that our response rate will be higher compared to doing a mail-out to the entire list. But it does NOT mean that 100% will buy. The model is predicting the likelihood, not guaranteeing it.

A more realistic prediction may be that people on this list are 'X-times more likely to buy than not'. Let's assume that among those in this 'highly likely' data-set, we find that 2,000 actually buy. Our numbers are then as follows:

Cost

3,000 x $2/mailer = **$6,000**

Let's take a moment to compare the two campaigns, without and with a Predictive Model. We can see a 33% increase in Revenue, but we see a dramatic drop in risk on the Cost side.

Revenue

2,000 x $500 Item Price = **$1,000,000**

Profit

$1,000,000 – $6,000 = **$994,000**

REVENUE	COST	PROFIT
$750,000	$100,000	$650,000
$1 M	$6,000	$994,000
33%	-94%	53%

The latter is what will really drive the growth of Predictive Modeling.

Companies are looking for ways to compete more effectively, which means they must be more discerning about where they invest their marketing dollars. Using a Predictive Model allows them to reduce their exposure to marketing campaigns that historically have more misses than hits. In one recent survey, companies turning to artificial intelligence as a means to create a profit wedge in their business model are seeing an '8.1x' increase in revenue and an '8.4x' decrease in cost.

Digging a little deeper into what a Predictive Model looks like, let's create an oversimplified version for illustrative purposes, if only to appreciate the enormous task Machine Language undertakes.

Many different models can be used to predict what someone

will do given a certain set of variables. Let's imagine that the aforementioned database expresses variables derived from the following content categories: demographics and online behavior, the latter drawn from the company's web analytics. Machine Learning would produce a linear model that may look something like this:

Demographic Variable Scoring

- Male 11.3
- Female 14.1
- Age Range (25–45) 10.7
- Marital Status 22.0
- Military 21.0
- Geographic Location 5.0
- Income Level 15.9
- Online Variable Scoring
- Search Term (Keywords) 17.1
- Newsletter Request 7.5
- Demo Request 25.5
- Download Whitepaper 17.3
- Number of Website Visits (greater than X) 5.0
- Page Views (greater than X) 10.0
- Browser 5.5
- Company Email 10.0
- Free Email (Yahoo, Hotmail, Gmail, etc.) 2.1

Based on the data it has and past results of various marketing campaigns, the Machine has assigned each variable a 'score' (i.e., the higher the score, the higher the correlation of 'will buy'). The Predictive Model would use a rule-based model to sort through the 'will or will not' buyers using simple heuristics (rules-of-thumb):

Rule 1: If the Demographic score is above 79.9

Rule 2: If the Online score is above 63.5

Rule 3: If the Demographic score is above 54.3

AND the Online score is above 45.2

In this example, anyone above the scores listed, or some combination thereof, would be considered 'highly likely to buy'.

Now, if these are existing clients, we can use historical data to generate more clarity about their willingness to buy.

- Past Purchase Variable Scoring
- Bought X Product 17.1
- Bought in the Last 90 Days 12.5
- Order Size (greater than X) 15.5
- Buyer Title: Purchasing, Buyer 12.3
- Bought with Credit Card 10.0
- Used Payment Terms 15.0
- Picked Up Purchase 5.5
- Frequency of Purchases in the Last 90 Days 10.0
- Annual Revenues (from credit application) 2.1

Now the Predictive Model starts to get a bit more complex:

Rule 1: If the Demographic score is above 79.9

Rule 2: If the Online score is above 63.5

Rule 3: If the Demographic score is above 54.3

AND the Online score is above 45.2

Rule 4: If the Past Purchase score is above 75

Rule 5: If the Demographic score is above 54.3

AND the Online score is above 45.2

AND the Past Purchase score is above 63

Rule 6: If the Demographic score is above 54.3

OR the Online score is above 45.2 AND the Past Purchase score is above 63.

I could add a few more permutations, but you get the idea. In this example, we are only working with 3 sources (i.e., de-mographic variables, social variables, and past history variables). Now imagine if we added a fourth database. A fifth. You immediately understand that for a mere mortal, keeping track of all the permutations becomes a logistical (rules) and mathematical (scoring) nightmare.

As we add more data sources, Machine Learning is able to take this information and reformulate a new Predictive Model with supervised learning (i.e., the results are applied as a feedback input to the machine, and corrective rules or actions are taken). Note that, in the present context, the 'supervised' in 'supervised learning' implies human agency in selecting and applying a given predictive output generated by the Machine, then collecting an observed result, and then applying that result as feedback to the Machine.

With this feedback mechanism in place, the Machine Learning component generates over successive iterations a series of model instances, each of which is a more accurate predictor than the previous. One might then ask, "Will this model converge to a point where not much correction is required?"

The answer is, "Yes." If our Machine is of sufficient power and sophistication, we'll soon arrive at a model we can trust, until the market changes. At that point, the learning process begins anew. Given that markets are always dynamic, a safe bet is that both 'we' and 'the machine' must keep learning.

The concept of Deep Learning comes into play when the machine autonomously seeks unrealized structure in the data and then develops Predictive Models based on any new relationships or patterns it might find. These algorithmic refinements are not programmed or hardcoded by any human agent. These are increasingly complex algorithms that the machine formulates on its own.

Think back to when you were learning to ride a bike. You had training wheels to stabilize your bike and an adult to provide the right nudge (left or right) and a push to keep you going. After a while, the adult would let go, and you rode the bike on your own. Later you learned how to 'pop' the front wheel up and ride the bike that way. At this point, your adult is no longer teaching you. You're improvising new 'moves' and learning on your own. This is a very loose description of Deep Learning, but you get the gist.

By construction, the Machine is learning to be 'creative' in finding new associations and relationships in the data to provide actionable insight you didn't see, or perhaps you observed the raw data but couldn't comprehend its deeper meaning.

What are some applications that we can use to sell more effectively in this hypercompetitive market? Well, we know that client retention is more of a predictor of business stability than client acquisition. In other words, keeping clients buying from us is a more certain way to grow the business compared to attempting to acquire new clients. With that in mind, here are some concrete applications of how Deep Learning can help us retain clients:

- **Cancellation:** What if we could predict ahead of time the likelihood of a client canceling? If we had this list of potential cancellations ahead of time, we could embark on some type of customer reinvigoration campaign. We would call the client and do a free, 1-hour consultation to answer any questions they might have, or we would schedule an onsite visit to uncover and address any prob-lems or concerns.

- **Renewal:** If a client is up for renewal, which clients need to be contacted to ensure they follow through? Let's say we are leasing broadband services to a large B2B company, and we want them to renew instead of opting for a competitor. The Machine would alert us about which clients are at risk of not renewing, and the salesperson would then reach out with a renewal discount or other customer appreciation incentive.

- **Upsell or Cross-Sell:** What if the Machine could predict which clients are ready to either upgrade their product or service (Upsell), or consider buying another product or service (Cross-Sell) the company offers? The customer wins because they are being offered something they need (but didn't ask for) or hadn't considered that anoth-er product might help them run their business more effectively. This is a so-called pre-emptive sales approach that, if done correctly, adds value to the customer experience.

Predictive Modeling gives companies the anticipatory power to take actions necessary to gain or keep their customer's business. Here is a short list of actions companies can take to retain, Upsell, or Cross-Sell an existing customer:

- Give the customer a call (i.e., the 'personal' touch)
- Offer a discount to show appreciation for their past business
- Send an email to touch base
- Send an offer via electronic newsletter
- Recommend a product they may be interested in
- Offer a free onsite review of how they're using the products they've purchased
- Send an invitation to a free webinar
- Schedule a lunch-and-learn

The list can go on, and I'm sure you can add a few suggestions of your own. The key point is that through Predictive Modeling, we can improve our chances of retaining clients by becoming more aware of those who might choose to take their business elsewhere.

In other words, Predictive Modeling sheds a light on those dark corners of our database where customers can get lost. The implied advantages are huge. In fact, if current trends hold (as they surely will), this technology will be essential in acquiring or maintaining a competitive advantage. Using Machine Learning to grow your business is not a matter of 'if', but 'when'.

When I hear skeptical managers dismiss Predictive Modeling or Machine Learning as technology outliers, I'm reminded of Plato's Allegory of the Cave. Plato describes a group of people who have lived their entire lives chained in a cave, facing a blank wall. The prisoners watch the shadows projected on the wall from objects passing in front of a fire behind them. These shadows are their only reality, the only world they know. One

47

day, some prisoners in the cave manage to break free and leave the cave only to discover that their reality, shadows on the wall, was not at all what they thought it was.

Those business leaders of a more 'traditional' mindset have been facing the cave wall, watching the shadows of the Information Revolution. This is what has shaped their various decision-making processes in recent decades. However, contrary to what they might believe, they've already reached the limits of spreadsheets and macros as an aid to their decision-making.

Today, the ability to see the 'angles' in any given market requires a higher order of intelligence to navigate, among other factors, a highly commoditized business environment. Artificial intelligence, in the form of a 'smart' Predictive Modeling capability, is breaking the chains that bind, and only those leaders who choose to leave the cave and see the new reality will succeed in the decades to come.

CHAPTER 5

The Upselling Mindset

Let's look at Marketing, but more specifically how Marketing thinks about business growth. Each year top management raises the bar for revenue growth. The Vice President of Sales gathers his sales team, managers and salespeople together for an annual sales review or conference where each territory or major account executive performs their 'here's where we're at and here's where we think we'll be next year' presentation.

Each presentation is delivered with a cautiously optimistic outlook and a muted enthusiasm that belies the reality. Each salesperson must walk the line of 'my territory shows promise' with 'but, it's not growing as fast as many would think' when doing their sales overview. No one wants to present too optimistically, and risk being handed down a sentence of an unexpected or, dare I say, unrealistic revenue growth number.

Meanwhile, the VP of Sales listens intently with an eye towards trying to figure out how best to distribute the new sales growth number.

After the territory and account reviews are concluded, the VP then hands down the revenue sentence, "Here's your new number." The verdict is usually met with incredulity by each team member, who then proceeds to protest as to why the new number is unreasonable, let alone achievable. The VP listens empathetically but in the end will tell them how much he be lieves in their ability to go out and find new business.

"I'm sure you'll be able to put together a plan for how you're going to hit that number."

Upon leaving the meeting, the sales manager (or salesperson) must now put together a plan to grow their business and the immediate go-to option is to find a way to gain new clients. The immediate questions are:

- Do I need to hire more people?

- How do we get more prospects in the pipeline?

- Can we go deeper into existing market (i.e., market penetration)

- What new market segments can we target (i.e., green field opportunities)?

- What new trade shows can we participate in to gener ate new leads?

- How can we get marketing to get us better leads (i.e., lead generation campaign)?

- How can marketing help us deliver more persuasive messages?

- What new products are being rolled out by product management that we can sell into new markets?

This is a great list of questions and I'm sure you can come up with a few more of your own. These questions focus on how to get more new accounts into the pipeline by requesting more resources to be able to go after new market opportunities. This is the go-to or default strategy of most companies and sales teams.

While gaining new clients is always a sound strategy for growth, it's not the only one. There are 4 ways to grow your business:

GAIN	**RETAIN**
GROW	**REACTIVATE**

Gain: This quadrant focuses on finding new markets and new clients. The strategies employed are usually identifying new markets and clients and putting together a go-to-market strategy with a combination of new marketing messages and/or hiring new people.

Retain: This quadrant focuses on a marketing outreach program to increase customer satisfaction by helping clients with tools and resources to enable them to grow their own business. Said another way, by adding value to our existing customers, they're more likely to stay than to go with a competitor.

Grow: This quadrant focuses on looking inward, as opposed to outward toward the market, at your existing client base to uncover other revenue opportunities by means of Upselling or Cross-Selling.

Reactivate: This quadrant focuses on two types of existing customers: infrequent and dormant. Infrequent buyers buy, but not as often as you'd like. The question then becomes, "How can we get them to buy more often?" Dormant buyers are those who haven't bought anything from you in a given time period (e.g., 1 year). The goal is to find out why and get them buying again.

It's my guess, and I think it's a safe one, when I say that some-where in the range of 80% of all sales growth plans are solely dedicated to the Gain quadrant.

It's worth highlighting here that getting referrals falls in the Gain quadrant. It's also worth further highlighting that while getting referrals is a great Gain strategy, it's also one of the most underutilized, as most companies simply don't have the process for acquiring referrals from existing clients.

The primary Gain or lead-generation activities are:

- cold calling
- social media connections
- participate in trade shows or events
- getting referrals
- ad spends

The above activities all have one eventual hurdle: you still have to get in front of a decision-maker who you don't person-ally know, let alone have a relationship with. This is why a Gain strategy is the toughest of the 4. Yet that's where companies focus. Why?

There's an embedded belief that if you aren't acquiring new clients or new market shares, then you're not really growing.

PORTFOLIO VS. WALLET

In business parlance, growing means selling more and that is usually the direct result of gaining new clients. Being able to add logos to your client roster is the goal of many. If you can sell to and capture a well-known company, that's a testament to your company and the products or services you offer. Getting new clients or growing your client portfolio is a good way of measuring penetration and market acceptance. Growth in this sense is quantifiable; number of new clients acquired each year.

But just counting new clients as a Key Performance Indicator (KPI) is only part of the overall performance of a sales team. If you were to submerge yourself in the minutiae of Client Acquisition Costs, you might see the following:

- What percentage of sales activities are lost on researching new clients?

- What is the Cost of Sale (COS) for a new client?

- What are the Margins on new clients?

- Not all clients are created equal. Have we acquired (demanding) clients who are a cost burden?

- How long are the sales cycles and how does it impact our COS?

- How many new salespeople were hired to go after new clients and markets?

- What are the training and opportunity costs associated with new hires?

- What are the marketing costs associated with implementing, executing and generating new leads?

The cost of acquiring new clients is usually bundled under the Cost of Sales (and Marketing), as it should be, but bundling obfuscates the time-sucking activities and associated costs. The COS is the metric everyone knows, but few really understand.

The COS is not only a money metric it's also a motivation metric. When salespeople are not motivated to sell, Cost of Sales usually goes up because sales efficiency goes down. Why wouldn't salespeople be motivated to sell? Well, it could be because:

- They just got nailed with a revenue increase (i.e., a new number) that they can't see how they can attain.

- They don't have the right tools to be more efficient at their job.

- They don't have a solid plan to hit their new number, let alone find new clients.

- They don't have the proper guidance to help them put together a winning sales strategy.

Telling salespeople to go out and just sell more is a directive, not direction. Telling salespeople to go out and find more (Gain) new business with the same resources they currently have is enough to demotivate. Salespeople need managers to guide them and help them formulate a plan to hit their number. Telling salespeople to go out, find new clients and grow your portfolio is not a plan, it's a wish. Salespeople need a believable plan, not just one loaded with New Year's Eve optimism.

Here are some questions for your consideration:

- What's more believable, that you can go out and find new clients or that you can get your existing client base to buy more?

- What's more believable, that you have easier access to new clients or existing ones?

- What's more believable, that your sales cycles will be shorter with a new client **or** with an existing one?

- What's more believable, that you can hit your new

revenue number by acquiring new clients or convincing existing clients to buy more of what you have to offer?

The mental shift salespeople, along with their managers, have to make is that hitting the new number can be done with acquiring new clients AND it can also be made that much easier by tapping into your existing client base and increasing your company's wallet share of the client's total spend. If a client spends X amount each year on a product or service you offer, then ask yourself the following:

- What percentage of that spend (budget)is my company getting?
- What can I do to increase that percentage?
- What new products or services can we offer to increase that percentage?

By asking yourself these different questions, you are now focused on how to get existing clients to buy more and what you need to do to get them to buy more.

Shifting your mindset from a Portfolio (How many clients do I have?) to Wallet (how much of the spend am I getting?) Share will allow you to focus on the immediate needs of a client who has demonstrated by past deals, that they a) are willing to buy from you, b) trust you, and c) would like to continue doing business with you. Why wouldn't you focus on a Wallet Share strategy to hit your new revenue number?

For example, let's say your company offers sales training services to a company. Aside from sales training, what else could you offer them? Here are some ideas:

1. Individual coaching services for salespeople
2. Consulting advice on specific or large deals

3. Sales research analysis on market competitors

4. Online learning platform for continuing education

5. Develop customized training programs

Again, you can choose to grow your Portfolio of clients or you can choose to grow your Wallet Share (i.e., Upsell) of existing clients.

THREE UPSELLING MOTIVES

It's easy to assume that clients know a lot about our products or services when in reality they only have limited knowledge as to what we as a company offer. That's why it's important to remind ourselves that we should never assume what the client knows or does not know. Upselling has 3 components that can add value to the customer experience by recognizing that the client may be:

- **Unaware** that an option (or opportunity) exists

- **Uniformed** as to what the options (or opportunities)

- Aware and informed of the options but views it as **Unimportant**

The value-add of Upselling can be found in making the client aware of an option or opportunity that they themselves didn't know existed.

Example 1: A new client has agreed to purchase an expensive printer for his business but may not want to use either his ex-isting cash or lines of credit. The client is unaware that your company offers financial options at competitive rates. At this point you can introduce your company's financial option as a third alternative to the purchase. Your company not only gets the sale, it also gets the interest on the loan.

Example 2: A client may want to purchase a software solution but is hesitant to commit to a monthly subscription, even though you have reassured him that he may cancel at any time. At this point you introduce an annual option with varying discount levels: 1 year option with a 10% discount and 2 year option with a 20% discount.

You want the client to say or think to themselves, "I didn't know you offered that!" or "I didn't consider that option!"

In some cases, the client is aware that the option or opportunity exists but is uninformed as to how they might benefit from it.

Example 3: You've decided to purchase a software package or application (app) to complete some specific task. What you didn't know was that there is an option that you can turn on for a small fee (Upsell) that will allow you to integrate it into all your other software applications making the user experience seamless.

Example 4: You've decided to buy a gaming platform for your video games, and you've settled on a set of specifications. The salesperson then informs you that for a few dollars more, you can purchase the exact same platform but with the option to upgrade in the future. The salesperson also informs you that new games will be announced at the end of the year that will require more speed and capacity.

You want the client to say or think to themselves, "I didn't know you could do that!" or "I didn't know that was going to happen!"

It's often the case that a client is aware of an option (or opportunity) and is well-informed but fails to see the importance in what you have to offer. This is usually the result of myopia or short-term thinking.

Example 5: Let's say you've sold a client on buying a custom designed pool. You attempt to sell the client on using a type of construction material that, albeit 10% more expensive, will prevent foundational cracks from forming. The client acknowledges the value and can see how it might be a good investment but decides against it. The salesperson runs the following scenario, "If you decide to sell this home in 10 years and the pool has foundational cracks, the cost to repair will be 20% - 30% of your pool's original cost, and if you forego the repairs, the ability to sell the house goes down dramatically. Better to spend a little more now, while we're constructing, than to have to pay later in time or money."

Example 6: A wedding event planner is working with the parents of the bride to pull off a beautiful wedding. The parents have reached their budget and have decided to forego a few items to stay within that budget. The event planner says, "I understand you want to stay under budget, but I would strongly consider adding a large tent reception area. If it rains, which could happen, I can't imagine all the guests fitting in your house. For a few dollars more, you can rest peacefully knowing that rain or shine, it's going to be a great wedding."

You want the client to say or think to themselves, "I didn't look at it that way." Or "I didn't think about that possibility!"

As a salesperson, these are the 3 questions you need to ask yourself after you've made the first sale and are looking to Upsell to the client:

- Are they aware that the option(s) exist?
- Are they informed of the options we have to offer?
- Do they realize how important these options are?

The Upsell mindset requires you to be mentally vigilant,

always surveilling your customer's business for new Upsell opportunities. Always having these questions constantly churning in your mind will allow you to discover new opportunities with your existing client base. Never take it for granted that they know what you have to offer or how important it might be to their business.

Now that your mindset has been firmly oriented towards selling existing customers more, let's talk strategy. Said another way, now that you have your 'why' Upselling is critical, let's talk about 'how' you're going to do it.

PART TWO

How to Upsell

UPSELLING STRATEGY #1

Freemium to Premium

The tastiest Freemium model I've encountered was at Costco. When you walk down the aisles of the warehouse you eventually encounter a food vendor who will offer you a free sample of food for you to try. If you like it, you'll probably buy it.

The word Freemium is a portmanteau of two words: free and premium. The objective behind the concept of Freemium is to get someone to try your product or service for free. The end goal is getting the client to use the product or service and decide to move to the next pricing tier or premium level and make a purchase in order to gain access to more features or benefits.

Most salespeople don't consider Freemium an Upsell strategy, but it is. Getting clients to try something requires that you sell them first on the idea that it is worth trying or using.

During the pre-Internet age, a similar strategy was used called the Puppy Dog Close. This sales strategy was aimed at first selling the client on the idea of taking the puppy home with the option of returning it in a few days if they weren't satisfied or happy. We can all imagine how that turned out in the majority of cases. Once the puppy was in the home, especially one with kids, game over. Freemium is an extension of this 'try it and if you like it' sales strategy.

The psychology behind Freemium is ownership. Once the client has the item in their possession, and likes it, the tougher it is for them to let it go.

TYPES OF FREEMIUM

Today's Freemium strategies go beyond just mere possession and center more around the concept of restricting clients from access to a high-order advantage. The first sale is still to get the client to try it for free, or a nominal price. Once they're 'in', you can apply different strategies which induces the client to Upsell themselves. Here are a few Freemium strategies you may have already encountered yourself and should consider using to Upsell more products or services:

Limited features: You can access and use the product, but you are limited from using the full set of features or capabilities. An example of this may be an online software product that allows you to use a video conferencing program but you are limited from using such features as screen-sharing, document sharing, or adding more than 1 attendee.

Limited capacity: You can use the service, but you are limited in how much of it you can use. For example, a podcast hosting company may offer you free usage for up to 1 GB per month. If you're a regular podcaster with a lengthy show format, this storage space may only be good for a few shows. You are now forced to consider moving your podcast to a cheaper hosting company or upgrading to the next level of storage.

Limited use license: You can create different licenses for different types of clients or usage rates. For example, if you wanted to use a royalty-free song on one of your promotional videos, you can do so for free as long as the video does not exceed a certain amount of views or downloads. Or, to avoid the hassle or anxiety of exceeding that number or someone else using the song, you can buy an exclusive (limitless) license.

Limited use time: This Freemium option is self-explanatory. If you want to use a product for free, you can do so within a given timeframe. Once the Freemium time has expired, you will be asked to make a choice between paying or letting your account expire. I'm currently using a software package that will expire after 10 days. Others I've used in the past expire based on the number of times you use (launch) the software application.

Limited support: If you want a particular type of support, you'll have to pay for it. Airlines use this strategy in a very subtle way. If you own a credit card with the airline's brand, on the back you'll find a special telephone number you can call to get faster access to customer support. For example, if you have an American Express card and switch to Delta Airlines' American Express card, you now have a Delta Number associated with that card, which will then be used to give you access to another tier of customer service. The more you fly with Delta using their credit card, the more points and privileges you'll receive.

Limited access: You can access content but are limited by some usage. The best example of this is the Harvard Business Review website, which lets you view 3 of their published articles per month. Once you've viewed 3, you will be asked to subscribe. If you don't, you simply have to wait for the following month before your article counter is reset to zero.

There are so many variations of how to use Freemium in order to get someone to try your products. Again, getting clients to try something for free is the first sale you'll have to make. The Upsell option comes into play when the client realizes the restrictions.

It's worth highlighting that we live in a world where we do not like limitations or restrictions on products or services. It's human nature to have a disdain for any thing that limits us from using the full feature set of a product. You can use this to your advantage when trying to get a client to buy more.

THE COST OF FREE

Even free has a cost and the Freemium concept uses that cost to its advantage. Allow me to explain. When a prospect goes online and decides to 'buy' something for free, they will be required to, at a minimum, give their email address. This will allow him to generate a login and proceed to use the product. Let's say in this case it's a free version of a Customer Relationship Management (CRM) system with limited features or functionalities for 30 days.

The prospect says to himself, "Well, let me see how easy it is to use and whether I like user experience."

The prospect then begins to invest his time in trying to understand the different things he can do within this limited free version. He proceeds to enter client information, revenue numbers, develop a sales process to track the status of a sale, connects to his email or social media accounts and even begins to generate re-ports from the user dashboard.

At the end of the 30 days, the prospect has to make a decision, buy or not buy. But now the decision is loaded with a different set of preferences and biases. At the beginning of the trial, the investment was an email, so the thought of not continuing after 30 days seemed a bit simpler. If I like it, I'll buy it. If I don't, I won't.

Thirty days later, the decision is not so simple. It's now more than just the per-month service cost. Now the prospect has to consider two other costs: sunk and opportunity.

In economics and business decision-making, a sunk cost is a cost that has already been incurred and cannot be recovered. In this case, the prospect has invested 30 days' worth of time in loading up the CRM with valuable data. If he decides not to buy the premium service, all that time and effort would be lost.

Another cost that has to be considered is opportunity cost. The prospect has already paid a price for his decision, his time and an alternative opportunity. When you decide to invest your time in one thing, you forego the ability to invest your time in alternative opportunity. That's an opportunity cost. If you decide to spend 3 hours playing video games, you've given up the opportunity of reading a book or learning a skill.

The prospect in this CRM example has invested count-less hours over the last 30 days, which means he has foregone the opportunity of using another CRM in that timeframe. If the prospect is considering not subscribing, part of that deci-sion-making process is the reinvestment of time in learning a new CRM product, reloading the data and foregoing some other opportunity (i.e., other things he could be doing with his time).

Let's take Facebook as another example of the Freemium model. I've invested not days, weeks or months, but years in loading my page with videos, graphics, commentary and I've connected with friends and family on the platform. For me to move to another platform would be mentally painful at this point. It's unimaginable to me to be able to port all my content to another platform. I've been enslaved by free. That's the genius of Facebook. They have a self-captured audience that is reluctant to leave because the opportunity cost is simply too high.

I currently use a Dropbox account to store all my videos, books, and podcasts. The service started out as free but as my consumption of storage increased due to the amount of social media content I am producing, I had to upgrade to the next level which, at the time, was about $50 per year for a given level of capacity. As I write this, my fee for next year will be $130 per year. I could buy my own hard drive and store the information there, but I would then have to transfer all my existing content to the new drive. That's painfully time consuming but possible. What isn't possible is accessibility. With Dropbox I can access my files from anywhere. A convenience I highly value. The alternative would be to carry my hard drive with me everywhere. First, that doesn't sound like fun, and second, what if I lose it? Do I have to buy another drive to have a backup for the backup? It all started out so innocently free.

Free is never free. There's always a tradeoff. And while there are some differences between a free trial and a Freemium model, both operate on the same principle: get them using it for free, then Upsell them.

The Freemium (free) to premium (paid) acquisition model works because it reduces the buyer's perceived risk upfront and focuses the buyer more on the upfront cost and not the sunk or opportunity cost associated with a trial (i.e., time invested).

UPSELLING STRATEGY #2

Multiple Options

Let's begin this Upsell strategy by first remembering that our brain is in constant surveillance mode and alerts us when there exists a contrast or a change in the environment. This is an evolutionary survival mode that has been with us since the early dawn of man.

Imagine yourself walking through a forest and you immediately notice a bush, 30 feet in front of you, starting to shake. Chances are there's something behind that bush. Whether or not it's dangerous remains to be seen. But upon seeing the bush shake, our body muscles tense up, heart rate speeds up, our blood is fully flowing, and our mind is keenly focused on what lies behind that bush. This combined physical reaction takes less than a second to engage.

The primal part of our brain is programmed for survival (life or death) and safety (mitigating risk). You have several options on which course of action you should take: go back the way you came, change direction (left or right), don't move (freeze), or go forward. With the exception of going forward (fight, no fear), the majority of times our brain will choose one of the other three options to avoid danger or, more precisely, to mitigate risk.

So aside from being a contrast detector, sensing a change in the environment, your brain is also a risk-mitigating machine. Your brain serves a dual purpose: to detect differences and to reduce the risk upon encountering those differences.

What does this have to do with Upselling? Before answering that question, let's visit a kitchen retailer, Williams-Sonoma, who planned to release a new bread making machine. The challenge, among many others, of releasing a new product in the market is determining the right price point to maximize profitability. The company already had at least 2 other bread making machines in the market. The sales were promising but fell short of expectations. It was surmised that the disappointing sales might be due to lack of name-recognition in the market. When a brand is unknown, without some type of reference to guide them, consumers will choose to 'mitigate' risk by either choosing a well-known brand or buying the lowest price model. This is key.

Back to the marketing plan. This new bread-maker would be the company's premium model, which meant it would have a higher price than the other model. The aim was to capture the high-end, luxury or status market that always enjoys buying the best.

After setting the price, the company just sat back, figuratively, and waited for the sales results to come in. Within a short time, they had their answer. Their bread maker sales increased dramatically, but not in the way they expected. Quite surprising, the premium bread maker sales were less than stellar, but the sales of the older model exploded.

Barbara Buell, over at the Standard Business, said, "Customers frequently don't know the value of products and must rely on comparisons set up by the retailer to determine if an offer is 'a good buy'. Williams-Sonoma used to offer one $275 home bread maker. Later, a second bread maker, which had

70

similar features except for its larger size, was added. The new item was priced more than 50 percent higher than the original. Not many of the new, relatively overpriced items sold, but sales of the cheaper bread maker almost doubled."[6]

Williams-Sonoma was able to increase sales of its $275 bread-machine by adding a second, larger model at a price of just over $400. There is no doubt that adding a more expensive model drove sales for the less expensive option. Why? Our brain is a risk-mitigating machine. When confronted with two options and it can't choose due to lack of name recognition or expected performance, the brain will go with the less expensive option (i.e., retreat to safety).

When consumers consider a particular set of choices, they often favor alternatives that are a compromise of their desired choice. This is called the 'Compromise Effect'. The compromise lies between what the consumer needs and what they can or are willing to pay.

So what does this mean to you? If today you're offering a product that isn't moving, you may want to consider adding a premium product or premium loss-leader to help sales. The higher price premium product acts as a price anchor or, more specially, as a frame of reference to help guide the customer in understanding what is cheap versus what's expensive.

The $400 bread-maker informed the customer that if they wanted the best of the best, that was the price. This price acts as the anchor or frame for a customer to be able to make sense of how much to pay. When the customer then sees the $275 option, they realize it is a less expensive model and they immediately calculate the saving in their head ($400 - $275 = $125). Now the buying questions shift from "Is this too expensive?" (when only

6. Stanford Business – The Limits of One-to-One Marketing by Barbara Buell.

the $275 option is available) to "Will spending $125 be worth the added features and benefits of the premium offering?" Said another way, having a premium product sets a price anchor and, by default, reframes the consumer's internal conversation from a pricing issue to which one is best (i.e., need and willing to pay) for them issue.

When presented with two options with little brand recognition, the brain will mitigate risk by choosing the less expensive option.

Let's say you own a furniture building company and you sell a special design of

Adirondack chairs. You currently have 2 designs you market: chair #1 is priced at $200; chair #2 is priced at $275. In a given year you sell 1,000 and 500, respectively. Total units sold equals 1,500.

Chair #1 = $200 Quantity Sold: 1,000

Chair #2 = $275 Quantity Sold: 500

Total Sales= $200,000 (1,000 x $200) + $137,500 (500 x $275) = **$337,500.**

As you enter a new year, you're looking for ways to increase your sales. You can invest in marketing. You can invest in building a better sales team. You can invest in expanding your sales distribution channels. All are great options. But a simpler, more manageable solution might be right in front of you if we apply the compromise effect again. What if we add a third, more expensive option? Your product offering now looks like this:

Chair #1 = $200

Chair #2 = $275

Chair #3 = $475

What do you think is going to happen? If you guessed that some will buy the premium chair option (#3) but most will settle in the middle (Chair #2), you are correct. The reasoning should be obvious by now. The middle option is viewed as a compromise between need and price, as already discussed. Also, keep in mind our primal instincts. Our brain wants to mitigate risk and will settle for something in between the extremes.

This isn't a theory, it's reality. It's a reality you see every day if you go to a fast food restaurant. They always offer you three choices: Small, Medium and Large. Go to Starbucks coffee and you'll be offered: Tall, Grande, Venti. If you buy services or subscriptions online, you'll notice the offer: Bronze, Silver and Gold (or Silver, Gold and Platinum). If you buy products, you'll be offered the Good, Better and Best options. These pricing structures aren't a coincidence, it's neuroscience and behavioral economics at work.

If we agree with or believe in the compromise effect, then in our chair example, we might see a sales distribution as follows:

Chair #1 = $200 Quantity Sold: 700 (was 1,000)

Chair #2 = $275 Quantity Sold: 750 (was 500)

Chair #3 = $475 Quantity Sold: 50

Sales (Revenue) Generated:

Chair #1 = $200 x 700 = $140,000

Chair #2 = $275 x 750 = $206,250

Chair #3 = $475 x 50 = $23,750

Total Sales = $370,000

That's a 9.6 % increase in sales compared to only having 2 chair options ($337,500 vs. $370,000). Keep in mind that the number of units remained the same (1,500).

PRICING ATTRACTION

Using options to drive a customer's perception of price is an effective Upselling strategy. You now know that when you offer a client 2 pricing options and you are an unknown entity (i.e., low trust), the majority of buyers will choose the lower price options to mitigate their risk. A rule-of-thumb I like to use is 60% - 40%, where 60% will choose the cheapest option and 40% will take a risk and buy the more expensive option. The percentage spread will vary depending on the situation and price points. The more expensive the options are, the more likely it is that the buyer will shift their preference to the cheapest or least expensive option.

With 3 pricing options, the majority of buyers will shift towards the middle option to mitigate risk. A good rule-of-thumb is 20%-60%-20% distribution, where 20% will choose the cheapest option, 60% will go for the middle (safest) option, and 20% will buy the most expensive option.

It's worth noting that there will always be a group of buyers who will want to buy the most expensive option. Their moti-vations may be driven by status (i.e., they always buy the best of the best) or, from their perspective, paying more is a way of mitigating risk. The driving belief for this group of buyers is, 'you get what you pay for'. This high-end buyer understands the opportunity cost of buying something that will eventually need to be replaced or upgraded. They'd rather spend the money now and not have to worry or think about their purchase fulfilling their needs. By buying the best, their perception is that they're buying security.

The brain mitigates risk at both ends of the purchasing

spectrum. Groups with little resources will buy the least expensive option. Groups with an excess of resources will buy the most expensive option. Groups in the middle have some, not many, resources and will shift towards the middle option.

All 3 groups base their decision on what to buy using price as an indicator of quality and benefit(s). As consumers, we've encoded 2 rules of thinking (i.e., heuristics) into our decision-making process:

- If it's expensive it must be superior quality.

- If it's inexpensive (cheap), it must be inferior quality

It's worth noting that when a vendor offers us a huge discount, immediately our primal brain senses that something must be wrong. Why else lower the price?

For price-hunters, a discount is a very appealing thing, but for buyers who have the resources to pay (i.e., high-spend buyers), a discounted price is going to make them more suspicious of your offering.

So it's fair to say that price has an attractive force associated with it. If you want to acquire Low-Spend Buyers, discounting is a good strategy. If you want to attract High-Spend Buyers, then selling with a discount is detrimental to closing a sale.

UPSELLING STRATEGY #3

Decoys

As already mentioned, when 2 options are provided, the client tends to buy the less expensive option. When 3 options are offered, the client tends towards safety (i.e., mitigate risk) and choose the one in the middle.

Now a twist. What if we wanted to shift the buyer from the middle option to the top, most expensive option? How would you do it?

To answer that question, let's turn to Dan Ariely, an Israeli-born professor at MIT in Boston, who wrote a fascinating book called *Predictably Irrational*. The book uncovers how irrational we are when it comes to decision-making, regardless of how rational we think we are.

The study of behavioral economics, how we make buying decisions, has exploded in the last decade. The drive to understand decision-making has been enabled by technologies like Functional Magnetic Resonance Imaging (FMRI), which allows researchers to look at the brain while decisions and preferences are being formed in near real time.

In his book, Ariely highlights how situational context drives our choices, not rationality. A classic example of how irrational we are is highlighted in his study of how we buy based on what options are presented to us, but more importantly, how those options are presented to us.

While price can be used to guide us to determine what's good or not, context can also be manipulated to drive our choices.

In one particular study, Ariely wanted to see how he could affect what type of paid subscription consumers would buy. For his test subject, he chose The Economist, an online resource (magazine) that offers authoritative insights and opinions on international news, politics, business, finance, science and technology.

In one of his many TED talks, Are We in Control of Our Own Decisions?, Ariely presents an ad from The Economist that offers two pricing options for subscriptions:

Web-Only: $59

Print and Web: $125

When presented with 2 options, and uncertainty lingers, the brain opts to mitigate risk and the majority of students went for the cheapest options. Most people (68%) chose the Web only option at $59. The rest (32%) chose the Print and Web option at ($125)

If one were to calculate the hypothetical revenue, based on 100 buyers, the numbers are as follows:

$59 x 68 = $4,012

$125 x 32 = $4,000

Total Revenue: $8,012

Ariely conducted a separate study using 3 options. But in this case, it was 3 options with a twist. Instead of 3 price points, he offered only 2 price points. Ariely asked a different group of 100 MIT students what annual subscription they would choose given these three options:

Economist.com Subscription	Economist Print Subscription	Economist.com + Economist Print Subsciption
$59	$125	$125

The results?

Web only ($59): 16%

Print only ($125): 0%

Print and Web($125): 84%

The hypothetical revenue, with 100 buyers, is as follows:

$59 x 16 = $944

$125 x 0 = $0

$125 x 84% =10,500

Total Revenue: $11,444

By adding the Print Only option at $125, the majority of buyers shifted to the Print and Web version, which was exactly the same price. The buyer's mindset shifted from $125 vs. $59 in the 2-option scenario to Print Only vs. Print and Web in the 3 op-tion scenario.

You can almost hear the buyer's thought process in the 3-option scenario: "Well, if I'm going to buy the print for $125 and it's the same as the print and web option, I might as well get both for the same price."

Simply adding the Print Only, or decoy option, revenues jumped 42.83%. While the decoy option is useless, it serves a purpose in influencing the buyer's decision-making process from bargain-hunting to maximizing their dollar to value ratio.

POPCORN EXAMPLE

Let's take a step back now that we have an idea of what the Decoy Effect is and how it can be used to shift a buyer's preference.

According to Wikipedia, "In marketing, the Decoy Effect (or attraction effect or asymmetric dominance effect) is the phenomenon whereby consumers will tend to have a specific change in preference between two options when also presented with a third option that is asymmetrically dominated. An option is asymmetrically dominated when it is inferior in all respects to one option; but, in comparison to the other option, it is inferior in some respects and superior in others. In other words, in terms of specific attributes determining preferences, it is completely dominated by (i.e., inferior to) one option and only partially dominated by the other. When the asymmetrically dominated option is present, a higher percentage of consumers will prefer the dominating option than when the asymmetrically dominated option is absent. The asymmetrically dominated option is therefore a decoy serving to increase preference for the dom-inating option."

If your head is spinning a bit after reading that definition, you're not alone. The best way to understand the Decoy Effect is to see how it can be applied in the real world with real examples.

If you've ever gone to the theatre to watch a movie and

decided to get some popcorn before taking your seat, I'm sure you were faced with the popcorn size dilemma. Should I get the small one or the large one?

At its essence, choosing popcorn size is a 2-dimensional decision where you have to take into consideration price and size. Yes, there are other human factors to consider, such as hunger and if you're alone or sharing with another person.

That aside, if price and size were the prime determinants in your decision-making process, how would you go about decid-ing which to buy if you were offered 2 sizes at 2 different price points?

The National Geographic Channel conducted an onsite study to see how the Decoy Effect affected a buyer's choice at a theatre[7].

During the first experiment, the customers approaching the snack counter were offered 2 options: a small $3 popcorn or a large $7 popcorn.

Large   Small

Not surprisingly, based on our previous examples, the result showed that the majority of consumers preferred buy-ing the $3 option over the $7 option. When interviewed after

7. The National Geographic Popcorn Experiment can be viewed here: na-tionalgeographic.com.au/videos/brain-games/the-decoy-effect-2400. aspx

making their choice, the consumers admitted that $7 seemed unreasonably high.

So, if in one evening of movie-watching 100 people ap-proach the counter and the majority, let's say hypothetically 80%, bought the smaller option, popcorn revenues would be:

Small Popcorn: 80 people x $3 = $240

Large Popcorn: 20 people x $7 = $140

Total Popcorn Revenue = $380 ($240 plus $140)

Then, a second study was conducted. This time, instead of being offered 2 options, the consumers were given 3 popcorn options: small $3, medium $6.5, and large $7.

Let's pause for a moment and analyze what's going on here. When a client is offered 3 options, the tendency is to migrate to the middle (mitigate risk) for safety. But, when the price differential between the middle and top (most expensive) is small, interestingly enough the decision shifts away from the cheapest ($3) option towards consideration between the $6.5 and the $7 option.

In this study, the majority of buyers chose the $7 option.

By inserting a decoy similar in price to the most expensive option, a buyer's attention was shifted upward.

When interviewed during the study, some participants said that spending an extra 50 cents seemed like a rational thing to do. Note again how the consumer's brain was subconsciously shifted from price consideration ($3 vs. $7) to context consideration ($6.50 vs. $7.00; it's only $0.50 more).

Let's run the numbers again but this time, let's invert the percentages with 80% now buying the large option and 10% each buying the small and medium options. Popcorn revenues would be:

Small Popcorn: 10 people x $3 = $30

Medium Popcorn: 10 people x $6.5 = $65

Large Popcorn: 80 people x $7 = $560

Total Revenue = $655 ($30 plus $65 plus $560)

By adding the medium-sized decoy at $6.5, popcorn revenue increased by 72.36% in this hypothetical situation.

Let's take a more modest purchase distribution of 20% small, 20% medium and 60% large. We would get the following:

Small Popcorn: 20 people x $3 = $60

Medium Popcorn: 20 people x $6.5 = $130

Large Popcorn: 60 people x $7 = $420

Total Popcorn Revenue = $610 ($60 plus $130 plus $420

In this case, total revenue for popcorn sales increased by 60.52% over the 2-sizes option.

RESTAURANT EXAMPLE

In another study conducted at Duke University entitled Adding Asymmetrically Dominated Alternatives [8], the researchers analyzed how buyers chose between alternatives in choosing a restaurant along 2 dimensions: star rating and distance.

For example, if you had 2 choices of restaurant to choose from, a 5-star restaurant with a 25-minute drive or a 3-star restaurant with a 5-minute drive, which one would you choose? The tradeoff here is between food-service quality of the restaurant (option A) and time-distance (Option B).

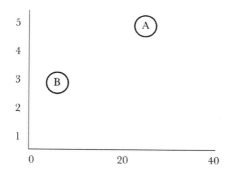

The researchers asked each study participant to make a choice based on their personal preference for quality or convenience.

Again, there are contextual deliberations that need to be taken into consideration. For example, if you're a person who enjoys quality food, you'll drive the distance. If you're pressed for time and it's rush hour, then you'll choose convenience.

---

8. Adding Asymmetrically Dominated Alternatives | Joel Huber, John W. Payne and Chris Puto I July 1981 | Duke University. Link: apps.dtic.mil/dtic/tr/fulltext/u2/al01132.pdf

That aside, the researchers now wanted to test the effects of a decoy on swaying the buyer's decision-making process. With a second group, the researchers gave them 3 options:

Option A: 5-star restaurant with a 25-minute drive

Option B: 3-star restaurant with a 5-minute drive

Option C: 4-star restaurant located 35 miles away,

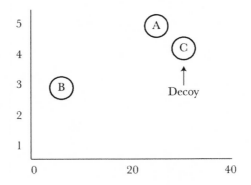

Option C is meant to act as an asymmetrical decoy in shifting the buyer's preference to Option A. And results showed that it worked. The majority of participants in this second group chose the 5-star rated restaurant.

By simply adding the 4-star rated restaurant (Option C) to the mix, it made Option A, the 5-star rated restaurant, more attractive in both quality and distance.

The researchers at Duke University weren't quite done. They wanted to see if they could shift the buyer's preference downward, toward Option B, the 3-star rated restaurant.

With a third group of participants, the researcher dropped the 5-Star rating (Option C) and inserted a 2-star restaurant that was a 15-minute drive.

Option A: 5-star restaurant with a 25-minute drive

Option B: 3-star restaurant with a 5-minute drive

Option D: 2-star restaurant located 15 miles away

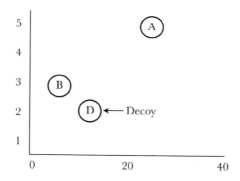

In this case, the majority of the participants in Group 3 chose the 3-star restaurant. The inserting of Option D shifted the asymmetric comparison (quality and distance) between itself and its 'nearest neighbor', Option B.

Now, how can you use this information? Well, if you're currently offering clients 2 options, it's worth considering how to apply the above strategies as a way to shift your buyers away from the lower price option to the more expensive one.

If you're offering an online subscription service, you can definitely use the decoy strategy to your advantage to shift the buyers upward. Much like The Economist example, you can offer your customers 3 options, where it's weighed towards the most expensive choice. For example, if you were to offer 2 options:

Option A (Includes features A-F) = $100 per month

Option B (Includes features A-W) = $180 per month

The immediate reaction would be the price differential being $80 and you would then do a quick benefit analysis to see if you really needed to spend more.

Now consider three options with a decoy:

Option A (Includes features A-F) = $100 per month

Option B (Includes features A-W) = $180 per month

Option C (Includes features A-Z) = $200 per month

In this scenario, you might go immediately to the middle option and then convince yourself that for only $20 more, you could have all of the features.

In real estate, for example, you can show the client 3 houses in similar price ranges, but one of the houses is in neighborhood A and the other 2 are in neighborhood B. Since A is the only house in that area, you as a consumer don't have anything to compare it to, whereas in neighborhood B, you can compare 2 options. Our brain will default into comparing the 2 houses in neighborhood B over the single one in neighborhood A. The agent has shifted the focus to neighborhood B.

Remember, your brain is a contrast machine. With no intrinsic understanding of value (i.e., what's good or bad), the brain will look to compare it with some reference point. The good news is that you can control that reference point by introducing a decoy into your pricing proposals.

UPSELLING STRATEGY #4

Endowment

As already discussed, we humans are irrational creatures. When we buy something, we value it. We give it a mental and a monetary weight. We love to own things and we hate to give up things. This tendency to attribute a higher value to things we own versus the things we don't own is called the Endowment Effect. This is a powerful human inclination that we can use to our advantage when Upselling a client.

One of the most often cited examples of the Endowment Effect is from a study by Daniel Kahneman, Jack Knetsch and Richard Thaler[9], in which participants were given a mug and then offered the chance to sell it or trade it for an equally valued alternative. In their studies they found that a person, once they owned the mug, was willing to accept no less than 2x the value of the mug. In other words, owning the mug (item) gave it twice the value than they were probably willing to pay for in the first place.

Say, for example, you saw a coffee mug you liked. You looked at the price, saw it was $3 and decided to buy it. A stranger then approaches you and offers y ou $3 for the mug y ou just purchased and you say, "No." If asked how much were you willing

9. Kahneman, Knetsch & Thaler (2009). Experimental Tests of the Endowment Effect and the Coase Theorem.

to sell it for, the price would likely be close to $6.

This is an example of Willingness to Accept (WTA), which is the minimum amount of money you are willing to accept to abandon your ownership of the mug. Ironically, if they were asked to pay $6 for the mug before owning it, they would probably reject the offer. Their Willingness to Pay (WTP) was lower than what they were willing to accept from a stranger once they purchased the mug. We are seriously irrational

The Endowment Effect is an explanation for loss aversion, a cognitive psychological term that states that consumers will move twice as fast away from loss as they would towards gain. We are twice inclined to avoid gain than to move towards gain.

From an evolutionary perspective, this makes total sense. If our primal brain is wired for safety and survival, and it is, the tendency is to protect what we have rather than risk gaining something we don't have. If a caveman is safe in a cave with a warm fire, he is less motivated to go out and risk the possibility of finding a better cave. Once you own it or have it, comfort in this case, giving it up causes your brain mental pain.

All this is to say that once you own something, you are less likely to want to give it up. In business, allowing a client to feel as though they own a product is a powerful way for them to attribute value (and emotional connection) to what you're offering.

What does this have to do with Upselling? Everything! As humans, and clients, once we own something, giving it up is difficult. Remember the Puppy Dog Close? The pet store owner would encourage you to take the dog home and if after a few days you wanted to bring it back you could. What's the catch, or should I say the mental catch? The seller (pet store owner) knows that once you take that puppy home, over time you will take mental ownership of the dog and there will be an emotional connection established, making it quite impossible for you to take the dog back to the pet store.

Here's another example of the Endowment Effect in action. Imagine for a moment that you have 2 groups of people in separate rooms and you want to run an experiment. You want to sell them a car, but you want to maximize how much each individual will pay for your car. So you run the following experiment with two groups.

Group 1: This group is told that they now own a car, fully loaded, with all the options. Let's say a fully loaded car would cost $75,000.

Instruction for Group 1: You give each group member an itemized list of all the added options (e.g., sunroof, customized upholstery, LCD displays in the headrests, augmented audio system, satellite radio, etc.), and their associated price. You then instruct each individual member to remove (cross out) any item they deem unnecessary or frivolous and submit the new price of their car. The final price for each member will then be added and divided by the number of members to arrive at an average.

Group 2: This group is told that they now own a car, with ONLY the most basic options. Let's say a basic (non-loaded) car would cost $55,000.

Instruction for Group 2: You give each group member an itemized list of all the available options (e.g., sunroof, customized upholstery, LCD displays in the headrests, augmented audio system, satellite radio, etc.), and their associated price. You then instruct each individual member to ADD any item they deem necessary and submit the new price of their car. The final price for each member will then be added and divided by the number of members to arrive at an average.

Which group do you think would have a higher average price, Group 1 or Group 2? If you guessed Group 1, you would be right. Why? In Group 1 the client was given the car loaded with all the options. They had taken mental ownership and their willingness to give up any option was that much harder. The pull of ownership was strong. Every time they had to part with something, it caused their brain mental pain. Which means that they were reluctant to give up anything, or at a minimum just a few things.

For example, if Group 1 consisted of 5 members, after each removed the unnecessary options, the price per member might be as follows:

Member 1: $67,500

Member 2: $63,000

Member 3: $71,000

Member 4: $69,500

Member 5: $73,000

Average Price: $68,800 ($344,000/ 5)

For Group 2, the condition was a bit inverted in that 'adding' more options than necessary caused them pain. The members in this group only owned the basic car and had NOT taken mental ownership of any of the added options. What they did own was the money in their pocket, and they were less willing to part with it for added options. Every time they thought of adding an option, it caused their brain mental pain.

For example, if Group 2 consisted of 5 members, after each ADDED the options, the price per member might be as follows:

Member 1: $57,500

Member 2: $60,000

Member 3: $59,000

Member 4: $61,500

Member 5: $65,000

Average Price: $60,600 ($303,000/ 5)

The fully loaded group had a higher average price ($68,800) than the basic model group ($60,600), because they were less willing to part with what they owned. Again, we value something more once we feel we own it. If told that you own them, you are less likely to give up those possessions (i.e., options). Loss aversion is a powerful persuader in getting customers to buy more without the apparent exertion of pressure. By giving the client the option to remove what they don't want, you are also giving them the illusion that they are in control.

LANDSCAPE PRICING

I know this strategy works because I was a victim of it. Even when I knew what the salesperson was doing to me, I couldn't resist the pull of the Endowment Effect.

My wife had been wanting to redo our backyard and she was not going to let the matter die on the financial vines. She wanted a combination of hardscape (tear up and replace our cement deck and pathways) and landscape (add trees, plants and shrubs).

I finally relented but at the same time I gave her a firm budget of $25,000 for the project. She agreed.

She then proceeded to do her research online and eventually found a company who looked to be a good fit for what we wanted to do. The salesperson came out to the property and sat down with us to discuss what we were looking for. His discovery process, asking key questions, was exceptional and I knew immediately I was dealing with a true sales pro. He asked us to step outside so we could walk the property.

As we walked, he asked a lot of questions with regard to our personal preference, meanwhile inserting his professional opinion on 'do's and 'don'ts'. It quickly became apparent that he knew his business. As we walked the property, he drew a mental picture of how the backyard could be transformed.

Once done, we walked back inside where he made us the following offer: "I'd love to work with you. We can have our design consultant come out and do a property walkthrough and then do a full-scale colored blueprint of your design based on the information you've given me. The process takes about two weeks. Then, I'll come back out to show you the final custom blueprint and we can add/subtract/modify as you see fit. The cost will be $2,500 for the walkthrough and blueprint design. If you decide to use our services, that amount will be subtracted from the final price. Can I go ahead and schedule an appointment for next week?"

We both felt good about his ability to deliver and decided to move forward.

Two weeks later the salesperson returned with a cardboard cylinder under his arm. My biggest hope was the he would stay within our budget. After revealing the design and walking us through it, he gave us 2 options:

Option A: $27,000

Option B: $45,000

Each option was a different design, yet each option contained something we wanted. It was apparent that the best option was Option B, which had 100% of what we wanted and then some. Option A had about 60% of what we wanted. Our attention almost immediately shifted towards Option B with my wife giving me the "What do you think?" look.

The salesperson, sensing our mental gridlock then said, "Look, it's apparent that Option B has more of what you want." He then slides the proposal and design our way, hands us a pen and says, "Why don't you take out what you don't need or want (from Option B) right now, and I'll go ahead and recalculate the price." Then he said, "I need to go to my car to get something. I'll be right back."

At that moment, I could feel the loss aversion kick in as my wife and I struggled to 'cross things off' the list of wants. In the end, we pruned it down to something we were both comfortable with, with the final price being $34,000. Nine thousand over our set budget!

How did that happen? When we saw the design, and saw how beautiful it looked, we immediately took mental ownership. Much like the fully loaded car example, it was hard to take things off the list. There's no getting around the fact that once you own an item, physically or mentally, forgoing it feels like a terrible loss.

When you're submitting a proposal, never start with the basic (low priced) option. Go with the fully loaded option.

When the client says, "That's more than I expected to pay, I don't have that in my budget or any variation of that," simply hand them the pen and tell them to go ahead and take out what they don't want and you'll go ahead and recalculate the price.

Bottomline, when it comes to shrinking a proposal to fit a client's budget, have the client do it themselves. Never cross things out for the client.

UPSELLING STRATEGY #5

Decision Fatigue

One of my clients, Michael Moore, owns a very successful pool company in Canada. Yes, I said a successful pool company in Canada. During one of my sales training sessions in Toronto, we got to talking about Upselling and the tremendous opportunity for growth that comes with putting together a consistent strategy.

Michael agreed that Upselling is under sold and under utilized. To illustrate his point, he told me about one specific client who he sold a pool to about a year earlier. The original design of their pool started around the $80,000 mark, but as the design and the client's needs evolved, so too did the price, which Michael eventually closed at $120,000.

I congratulated him on his ability to adapt to the client's needs and his ability to Upsell the client. Michael, responded, "I was pretty impressed with myself until I spoke to one of my colleagues in the pool business who also sells patio furniture. Come to find out this same client bought an additional $30,000 in patio furniture from him a few months after the pool was complete."

I asked him, "Why do you think she decided not to buy the patio furniture from you?"

"I don't know. Maybe because I thought at the time she had bought as much as she could afford or was willing to buy."

I said, "Apparently not."

Michael paused for a moment to give the question more thought and then blurted out, "I think maybe she had decision fatigue." Michael was on to something.

Decision fatigue refers to the deteriorating quality of decisions you make after a long period of decision-making. If you've ever had to make planning decisions for an important event you know what I'm talking about. If you've ever gone to a dealership to buy a car and are confronted with the endless options and features, you know what I'm talking about. If you've ever had to plan an exciting vacation for your family, you eventually get to a point where you're not thinking about the quality of the decision, you just want to make decisions and be done with it. As I write this, my daughter is in the process of planning her wedding. I can tell you with certainty that she is burned-out on making decisions and needs a break from thinking about it.

Decision-making takes mental effort and energy. It requires that each decision be evaluated on the merits of cost versus benefit. Yet some decisions are easy while others require a careful analysis regarding cost and consequences.

In weightlifting, you can exhaust yourself 2 ways: lift something excessively heavy and do a few reps; or lift something light and do an excessive amount of reps and sets. The latter is a great analogy for having to make too many decisions. Initially, the decisions are easy, and your brain can execute (do the mental reps) easily. But as you move on and do more reps of decision-making, decision fatigue, much like muscle fatigue, begins to affect your performance.

Decision fatigue can lead to a client making poor choices about their purchases. Aware of this, clients simply stop making decisions altogether. Which is what I suspect happened with Michael's client. Put yourself in the client's position for a moment and imagine how many decisions go into the construction of a new pool like planning, design and material choices.

Michael's company builds an average of 350 pools per year. If we multiply 350 x $30,000 in missed sales, that's $10,500,000 ($10.5M) of Upsell opportunity that wasn't captured. If we believe Michael, regarding the client having decision fatigue, then what can we do as salespeople to capture those sales?

If one were to plot out decision fatigue against time, the chart might look something like this:

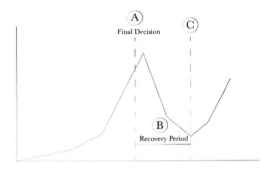

Reference Point A: This is where the client reaches decision fatigue and decides to end any further decision-making.

Reference Point B: A client requires a certain span of time from making any decisions before being able to re-engage. We'll call this the recovery time span.

Reference Point C: Although the client is ready to make more decisions, you'll observe the decision fatigue is not at zero. The client may be ready to make new decisions but it's worth being aware that some fatigue still exists.

Let's go back to Michael's client. The original price point was $80,000. As Michael shared more value with the client, the price point went up to eventually hit $120,000. That's a 50% Upsell. The good news here is that Michael closed on the first sale and then managed to Upsell the client.

The only thing Michael missed was realizing that it wasn't that the client didn't want to buy more from him, the client had simply reached Point (A) on the decision fatigue curve. To cap-ture those additional revenues, you first must be aware that the client has reached decision fatigue and you need to have a fol-low-up or Upsell process in place.

Let's begin with awareness. How do you know a client has hit decision fatigue during the sales process? We can start by looking and listening for signs.

Visual cues:

- Less eye-contact; looking down or away more

- Distracted with other things around them

- Fidgeting in their chair or, if standing, they shift their weight impatiently (or rock).

Verbal cues:

- "These choices are overwhelming."

- "Just show me the top 3..."

- "Too many choices to pick from."

- "Can you repeat why one is better than the other?"

Usually, it's not so much what the client says, but how they say it. Pay attention to a client's tone, which may sound impatient or irritated. The client may snap back after you present an option and say, "Yeah, yeah, that's good enough" or simply give you a short but firm "No".

If you've detected that you've reached the client's limit of decision-making (Point A), then it's time to back off and shift the conversation towards something less taxing so you can end on a positive note and make the client's buying experience feel good.

It's good to keep in mind that clients remember the beginning and the end of an experience, so make sure you end on a high, in the case of selling a pool, note of excitement about how much they're going to enjoy it and the memories they're about to create.

Now, let's talk follow-up and timing. With a sale this big ($120,000), the client simply might not want to make any more decisions until the construction of the pool has started or is nearly complete. This makes perfect sense from a client's standpoint who (a) has just spent a lot of money, and (b) will be observing how diligent and timely you'll be during the construction process.

At some point during the latter stages of the construction, the client can begin to see that the pool is nearly complete. Enough time has passed (Point B) and now the client should be open to making a new set of decisions (Point C).

As part of Michael's sales process, he can begin to implement a '30-Days Before Completion' trigger in his Customer Relationship Management (CRM), Enterprise Resource Planning (ERP), or Project Management system.

At this point Michael could setup a follow-up call with the client at their home to answer any lingering questions or deal with any minor issues. During this visit, Michael could then offer the client some patio furniture options.

Now that the pool is completed, the client can visualize what they'll need for the pool. And who knows, seeing what they need, Michael may be able to sell them more than the $30,000 they bought from his colleague. That's why a second sale after some time has lapsed or a follow-up is key.

Lastly, it's worth mentioning that this Upsell opportunity could have been misdiagnosed altogether. Maybe the problem wasn't decision fatigue but more about storage. Maybe the client didn't want to buy the patio furniture until the pool was complete to avoid having to store it. In this case, Michael could've easily offered to 'store' the patio furniture for the client until the pool was built and have it delivered upon completion. "Bill, what we can do is hold the patio furniture in stock for you and then have it promptly delivered when the pool is complete. That way there is no delay and you can enjoy your pool immediately."

Upselling is more than just selling. It's adding value to the buying experience. Salespeople think that Upselling is a way of driving more company revenues, and they are not wrong. But that's only half of the picture. When you expose a client to other options, you shift their perspective in terms of what they thought they wanted or needed. By offering the client options they hadn't considered, you are also enhancing the customer experience.

There are few things worse than buying something for your enjoyment and then realizing it's missing a critical piece or, worse, for a few extra dollars you could've had exactly what you wanted and needed. Clients are willing to buy more if it furthers their initial desires and intent (e.g., enjoy the pool and with their family).

UPSELLING STRATEGY #6

Downsell to Upsell

A key aspect of successful Upselling is gaining or earning the trust of your client. Trust is the new currency in an age where the choices are endless and the possibility of choosing wrong can cost a client dearly in terms of time and money.

From the client's side of the table, finding a trusted seller of products or services is something we all covet as consumers.

For the last 15 years, I've been taking my car to the same shop run by a man named James. James's car and collision service focuses on foreign automobiles. I found James after I felt I was being taken advantage of by my local car dealer where I usually took my car. I got suspicious after the third time I took the car in for an oil change. I started to notice a pattern. Every time I took my car in for a simple oil change, I'd go to the waiting room to wait for the service to be completed. About 30 minutes later, a service person (mechanic) would call me to the counter to in-form me that while in the process of doing an oil change, they also took the opportunity to run a few diagnostics as a courte-sy. And, after running the diagnostics they found a few things I should consider doing to the car while they were 'in-process' with the car. The dialogue always seemed to follow the 'Diagnostic - Question - Our Records - We Recommend' sequence. And every time I took my car in for an oil change, without fail I'd walk out of there spending way more than I expected.

The straw that broke this camel's back was the last time I was there. Here's how that conversation unfolded:

Service Person: "Victor, go ahead and get yourself some water or coffee in the break room and we should be done in about 30-40 minutes.

About 30 minutes later, the service person returns and calls my name.

Service Person: "Victor, since we had the car up on the lift, we thought we'd run a few diagnostics as a courtesy. (Diagnostic)

Victor: "Uh, okay."

Service Person: "When was the last time you replaced your fan belt?" (Question)

Victor: "Um ... I don't really know."

Service Person: "Well, our records show they haven't been replaced. (Our Record)

Victor: "Uh, okay."

Service Person: "We recommend that all belts should be replaced every 50,000 miles. Should we go ahead and do that?" (We Recommend)

Victor: "How much will that cost?"

Service Person: "With parts and labor, it would be $179.95."

Let me pause this story for a moment here. What triggered me to take my car in was that (a) I was reaching the 3,000-mile mark from my previous oil change, and (b) I received a 'special offer' of 30% off an oil change, which meant the oil change would only be $39.99. Heck of a deal if you ask me! Now I was looking at $235 ($39.99 plus $179.95 plus 7% tax). Hold the phone!

Back to the conversation.

Victor: "Uh, did you inspect the belt or are you just going off the record?"

Service Person: "What do you mean?"

Victor: "I mean, is the belt damaged or visibly worn?"

Service Person: "Uh ... I don't know. I'll have to ask the mechanic."

Victor: "So you're just going off the record?"

Service Person: "Uh, yes."

Victor: "So when you said you ran a diagnostic, what did that include?"

Service Person: "Oh, we hooked up your car and everything looked good. But I just thought I'd pull up your service record to see what had been done to the car."

Victor: "Okay. So before I decide to buy the belt, can you confirm with your mechanic that it needs (emphasis added with a harsh tone) to be replaced?"

Service Person: "Sure."

Moments later ...

Service Person: "The mechanic says the belt still looks good, but I would strongly recommend replacing it. The last thing you want to happen is for the belt to fail during a long trip or something.

At this point the service person was shifting from 'need' to scaring me into buying the belt by raising the specter of what would happen if I'm on the road on a dark, cold lonely road. I felt manipulated.

Victor: "I think I'll just hold off for now and just go with the oil change."

Service Person: "Okay." (In a 'you'll be sorry' tone.)

I drove home irritated.

As I pulled into my driveway, I saw my neighbor John, who I've known for 15 years, and I've come to trust him. John has proven time and time again that when he refers someone, you're going to get a high-caliber professional and a fair price.

I told him what had happened and asked if he knew of a better place to service my car. And that is how I found James.

The next time I decided to take my car in for an oil change, I set up an appointment with James. I took the car in and waited in the waiting room. Thirty minutes or so later James calls me up to the counter and says, "Victor, your car is ready."

What? No Upsell? Not pitch on what I 'should' do?

I asked, "So you found nothing else wrong with the car?"

James: "Well, we hooked it up to the machine and other than the AC filter being a bit dirty and may need to be replaced next time, the car looks great."

At this point I told James about what the service person at the dealership told me.

James said, "Well, I looked at it myself and they looked perfectly fine to me. Like I said, the only thing I found was a dirty filter, which still has some life in it."

James didn't try to Upsell me on what else he thought I needed. In fact, he Down-Sold me on what I needed by telling me eventually I'll need a filter (an Upsell), but not now (a Down-Sell). With that conversation, James earned a loyal customer for life.

You see, every time I take my car in, I feel like I'm dropping it off with someone who cares about it as much as I do and isn't reaching into my pocket to grab my credit card. James has earned my trust and, along with that, credibility.

For example, when James eventually recommended I put in a new belt, I did it. And here's where James differentiated himself and his business. After swapping out the belt, he had it waiting for me on the counter for me to inspect for myself. James then took a few moments to show me and highlight the stress areas of the belt and educated me on when you know it's time to replace them.

When you earn a client's trust, you've earned something more valuable than an Upsell: lifetime value. Over the years there have been times when I've taken the car in and James would call me to the counter to inform me that other things have to be done. And, whether or not James realizes what he's doing, he's using a Down-Sell strategy to Upsell me. He Down-Sells me on what's not urgent, Upsells me on what is urgent, and lets me decide.

For example, one time I took the car in for a major repair (e.g., get my tires changed, alignment and rotation). Later that day, James called me to tell me that there are a few other things that he found when he had the car up on the lift. He then told me 'the what', 'the why' and the 'how much' for each of the repairs or maintenance. He then offered his 'must do' and 'can wait' recommendations, and let me decide. "You must do these two things, this third thing can wait, but eventually you'll have to do it. So either bite the bullet now, or you can wait until the next time you bring it in. What would you like to do?"

Nine times out of ten I'll tell him to go ahead, never questioning the price or the need. His Upsell strategy is to only sell you what needs to be done and he Down-Sells you on what can wait.

Down-Selling is counter-intuitive. It catches a client off guard. Down-Selling temporarily confuses a client who is accustomed to someone trying to sell them more, not less. Again, this isn't about manipulating a client to gain their trust with the long-term goal of taking advantage of them. The Down-Sell to Upsell is about building trust upfront with your client. Letting them know you are looking out for them and their wallet.

I estimate that over the last 15 years I've spent an average of about $800 a year with James. That's a Customer Lifetime Value (CLV)of $12,000 ($800 x 15), so far. Over the years I've touted his service to anyone who has ever felt the money grip of some car dealerships. Friends of mine now use James and also sing his praises. I'm sure, in some small way, I've contributed to reducing his Client Acquisition Cost (CAC).

The surest way to earn a client's trust and respect is to sell them only what THEY need or will need, not what you WANT them to buy. Do that, and eventually your client will WANT what you want for them. Down-Sell to Upsell is a long-term financial win-win.

UPSELLING STRATEGY #7

Below-At-Above

Another strategy you can use to build trust before trying to Upsell a client is a 3 option approach with a Down-Sell. Let's suppose you've decided to go on the biggest vacation of your life with your partner. You've decided on a European tour that will last a month and you'll be visiting 9 different countries. You reach out to a highly recommended travel agent and you describe what it is you want. The fact that the agent is highly recommended already comes with a certain level of trust. You inform the travel agent that the budget for both of you is $40,000 and you describe in great detail what it is you both want out of the trip.

With your objectives well documented and your budget set, the agent says, "I completely understand what you're looking for. Give me a couple of days to put something together."

Before you get off the phone you remind the agent one more time that $40,000 is the budget you're working with. After getting off the phone, what would be your thought if this were you? You'd probably be thinking, He's going to go over that budget, I know it. You wouldn't be alone.

Three days later the agent calls you up and asks if you have a moment to talk, "I've put together some options for you, are you available to talk?'

"Absolutely."

The agent then goes on to describe what he's put together. Meanwhile, you're going through your mental checklist to make sure all the excursion highlights are included. At the same time your brain is screaming, "How much? How much?"

"Well, I've put together three packages for you." continues the agent. He then goes on to describe the Deluxe, the Master and the Standard packages.

"The Deluxe all-inclusive package is $45,000 and that includes business class airfare, 5-Star hotel, and any amenities." Your immediate mental reaction will most likely be, 'I knew he wouldn't stay within budget. He's just trying to Upsell me to earn a bigger commission.' Again, you wouldn't be alone in your thinking.

He continues. "Now, our Master package includes everything the Deluxe has to offer with the exception of business class airfare, you'll have standard seating for your flight. If you're okay with that, then the price is $40,000, which is within your stated budget." Your brain breathes a sigh of relief upon hearing those words and you can already see yourself on vacation.

"The third package is the standard package with all the excursions, standard airfare but instead of a 5-Star hotel, you'll be staying at 3-star hotels with no amenities and that package is $33,000, which is $7,000 below your stated budget," he concludes.

If you were the client, what would you be thinking right now?

Deluxe	$45,000	Business Airfare, 5-Star Hotel
Master	$40,000	Standard Airfare, 5-Star Hotel
Standard	$33,000	Standard Airfare, 3-Star Hotel

My immediate reaction to this would be one of pleasant surprise since in the majority of cases where we ask for a proposal with options and give the salesperson a budget, they usually come in way over budget, which unfortunately seems to be standard practice.

In this particular case, your initial thoughts might be, Wow! He actually found something at and below our budget. I like this guy.

The Standard (below budget) option transmits to the client that you are looking out for their best interest (i.e., spending). Clients connect with people who understand their pain points. This couple may have been saving up for years just to take this dream vacation. The last thing they want is for someone to oversell them and make them spend more than they deem necessary or reasonable.

The below budget option of $33,000 acts as a pattern interrupt (i.e., catches the buyer off guard) when compared to the standard package. A below budget price is unexpected as many salespeople would want to push a higher price to earn a higher commission.

The Deluxe (above budget) option represents the other end of the spectrum in terms of quality and price. This transmits to the client that you not only understand them but respect them enough to give them the option of buying the best of the best.

Too often we look at a client and prejudge how much they're willing to spend and, as a consequence, only offer them options in and around their stated budget. By providing the client with the best of the best option, albeit over their budget, you demonstrate that you want them to at least have the option of knowing what that package looks like and let them decide. You're not prejudging how much they're willing to spend and you're also letting them know what's possible for a little more money. Giving people the option to buy more opens them up to considering what they otherwise wouldn't consider.

The Master (at budget) option is the one they'll initially focus on because it's within their stated budget. The moment you present the at-budget option, the brain immediately feels a sense of relief and calm. The brain goes from anxiety to certainty in an instant and the client feels good. That good feeling is then attributed to you, which helps build the bond between you and the client.

Now, which option will they choose? For the answer, let's look at the four possible pricing scenarios:

Pricing Scenario #1:

Deluxe: $45,000 vs. Standard: $33,000

It's safe to say that if these two options were presented, the majority would probably go with the Standard package as a $12,000 difference is hard, not impossible, to justify. If the budget is $40,000, the couple would probably think, That's $7,000 under our budget, we could use that as spending money on our trip.

Pricing Scenario #2:

Master: $40,000 vs. Standard: $33,000

In this case the majority would probably go with the $40,000 option, especially if they're leery of what 3-Star hotels might mean in Europe.

Pricing Scenario #3:

Deluxe: $45,000 vs. Master: $40,000

This option would be a toss-up depending a lot on the client's preference for comfort when it comes to air travel. For example, a tall person would probably go with the Deluxe option. I would also venture to guess that if it were an older, well-to-do couple going on the trip, they'd also go with the Deluxe package.

Now, in the popcorn example, you'll recall that by inserting a decoy price option ($6.50), we can shift the client's attention to the middle and higher priced ($7) popcorn (i.e., away from the $3 popcorn). The client does all the rationalization, "For only $0.50 more, I can get the large." The same logic applies in this fourth hypothetical pricing proposal.

Pricing Package #4:

Deluxe: $45,000 (Business Airfare, 5-Star Hotel)

vs. Master: $40,000 (Standard Airfare, 5 Star Hotel)

vs. Standard: $33,000 (Standard Airfare, 3 Star Hotel)

I'm sure you can see that the Master (at budget) option is the decoy. In this scenario, with the at-budget price, the decoy has a dual role: shift the client's attention towards the Deluxe and build credibility and trust by being at the client's budget point.

The client is relieved that the agent was able to find a reasonable option at-budget. This puts the client at ease. Then, the client begins to consider the Master option and thinks, You know, for only $5,000 more we could travel in luxury on our big trip. It's a bit more than we expected to pay, but for a once in a lifetime trip, it might be worth it. We owe it to ourselves to make the best of this trip.

At this point the client is selling themselves. You don't really have to sell. The decoy (Master) option is doing all the work for you. The only thing you need to do is 'nudge' and guide the client's decision-making process by mentioning things they may not be considering at the moment. You could inject comments like this in the conversation:

- "If you're planning on bringing carry-on luggage, it might be difficult. The Standard package doesn't come with priority boarding, so there may not be overhead space available when your group boards."

- "This particular plane, coach (standard) class has very narrow seating and 18" of legroom, which is quite tightfor a tall person."

- "A 30-day trip is very grueling. On the way back you're going to be extremely tired and as anxious to get back home. So although comfort doesn't seem like a priority now, it might be on the way back."

Using the below-at-above Upsell strategy is the Decoy strategy with an 'at price' option for the client to earn or gain their trust. As clients today are more suspicious than ever when it comes to salespeople trying to oversell them, it's important to demonstrate empathy (i.e., understanding their mindset). At-pricing makes it clear that you are putting their ability to save money in front of your need to make money. And that's a big trust-builder.

UPSELLING STRATEGY #8

In-Return Upsell

One of the scenarios every salesperson encounters is a buyer or client asking for a discount. The deal was so close to being done and at the last minute the client wants you to sweeten the pot by giving them a price discount. Oftentimes the client will also remind you that your closest competitor is willing to give them a better price. This is tantamount to buyer blackmail, "Give me a better price or I'll take my business elsewhere."

Giving a client a discount can be a short-term fix to close the deal, but it can also become a long-term problem. For example, giving a client an innocent 5% discount may not mean much at the moment, but the next time you're in the same situation (i.e., ready to close a new deal), the client's pricing mindset is already taking into account the 5% discount you gave them last time. Negotiation starts from there. The client will ask for another 5%. You capitulate one more time and say, "Okay."

Depending on your cost (fix and variable) structure, a 10% discount could impact your margin anywhere in the range of 20% - 30%. Most salespeople never think about it from this perspective. They see a 10% discount as just that, 10% off. It's usually much more than that. Add to that fact that if you give a 10% discount, you'll have to make up that 10% elsewhere by selling an

112

existing client more or finding a new client altogether. In other words, a discount doesn't just have a monetary component. It also contains a time component.

So, when a client asks for a discount, because the price is too high or not in their budget, instead of giving them a discount, there are several things you can do to counter the request:

Discount Countermove #1: Remove a line item. If the client is buying a list of things, have them remove an item. The keywords here are 'have them'. Do not remove the item for them and then re-approach them with a new proposal. Instead, hand them the proposal and then have them take out what they don't really need to get the price down to within their budget. "Mr. Client, I understand. I'll tell you what, why don't you go through the proposal one more time, take out what you don't need right now, and I'll go ahead and recalculate the price." (Slide the proposal over with a pen or, if you're using a laptop/tablet,turn it in their direction.)

Discount Countermove #2: Propose three options (Good, Better or Best). If the client wants the Best solution but it's outside their budget, nudge them down to the Better option. "Mr. Client, I understand that the Best option may be out of your range, so let me suggest you go with the Better options instead."

Discount Countermove #3: Offer them a substitute product or alternative that is at a lower cost to bring the overall price down. "Mr. Client, if price is really an issue, we can swap out Product X for Product Y. It will do almost everything you need, and it'll bring down the price to fit your budget."

Discount Countermove #4: Offer the client 'used' items. You often see this at electronic stores where a used or returned item is repackaged and offered at a discount from the original price. The product is still new, it's only that the previous owner changed their mind for some reason. "Mr. Client, we also offer the same model that was previously used (returned). The product is almost new and is XX% less than the new product. Again, the only difference is that it has been opened or used for a brief time."

Discount Countermove #5: Offer the client a free service. Instead of giving a discount on a product, offer them something for free, like training or access to an online academy where they can learn how to use a product or solution. "Mr. Client, while I can't discount the product, I could offer you free training. We have an online academy that helps clients learn how to use and maximize the features of our product(s). The academy is normally priced at $X,XXX, but I'll go ahead and include it." The interesting thing about this option is that many clients who do agree to the terms end up never actually using or taking the training. In the gift card industry this strategy is called Breakage, which simply means that not all of the money on the card will be redeemed. If you give someone a $10 card and they only use $9.25 of it, they'll most likely not use the card again to claim the $0.75. The gift card industry banks on that. A small amount like $0.75 might not be much. But multiply it by 1 million cards and the number becomes significant. When you offer the client free training to close a deal, if they don't use it, that's Breakage (resources never used) in your favor.

Discount Countermove #6: Offer the client a loss leader. A loss leader is typically a product that has thin margins and isn't really moving (i.e., selling well) that you can use as a giveaway to entice the client to buy another product or service. For example, if you're selling a software platform, you may throw in the cost of a hosting service (cloud) as part of the deal. As a percentage of the overall deal, the cost of the server may be negligible. "Mr. Client, instead of a better price, what I will do is include in your package a cloud hosting service with the following specifications so you can immediately run our software without the need for any other resources. This has an annual value of $X,XXX. I'll go ahead and include that as a show of good faith."

Discount Countermove #7: Give the client financial options or terms. In a given situation, the client may already be willing to buy but the payment terms may be a little more than they have budgeted, which is why they're asking for a discount. Instead, you offer them better payment terms. For example, your current payment plan is Net 30 (i.e., pay this off in 30 days). "Mr. Client, I understand the need to stay within your budget. I have a win-win solution. Why don't I go ahead and change the payment terms in your favor? Instead of Net 30, let's do Net 90, which will give you more time to work the budget."

In all the above scenarios, you've protected the integrity of your product's value by not devaluing it with a discount. Bravo!

But we know that life and clients aren't always so compliant or predictable. There will be times where you'll have no choice but to give them a discount if you want to win the business. If that's the case, then you still have one final option that you can use to win the deal; ask for something in return.

Discount Countermove #8: Ask for something in return. If a client insists on a discount or price break, then you have the right and moral ground to ask them for something in RETURN. For every concession you make, you should insist on getting something in return. Here are three things you can do to get something in exchange for a discount:

1. Increase volume: This is where you ask the client to increase the volume or number of units they are currently willing to buy. For example, let's say you're selling a production widget and the proposal on the table is $50,000 for 1,000 widgets (unit price = $50 per widget). You say, "Mr. Client, if you could increase your order to 2,000 widgets, I can reduce the unit price by 10% or

$45 perwidget, which would bring the total order to $90,000 ($45 multiple by 2,000). How does that sound?"

2. Increase average order size: Similar to increasing thevolume of the order, sometimes it's easier to ask for abigger order. For example, the client has a $50,000 budget and is buying many items. Discounting across the board is not an option. "Mr. Client, if you can increase your budget to $65,000, I'll be able to increase the quantities of these items and I'll include at no cost to you the following options (e.g., free online training, loss leader)."

3. Ask for an extended contract: You may be in a situationwhere every year you have to renegotiate a contract. If the client asks for a discount of, say, 10%, you'll say, "If we can extend the contract for 2 years, I can get my management to sign off on a 10% discount across the board."

By asking for something in exchange for a discount, you condition the client to understand that you will always ask for something in return. This in turn may prevent them from asking for any future discounts.

The goal is to avoid discounting any way possible. Discounting to win business is not selling, it's gifting value and not getting anything in return. Use the 8 discount countermoves above to push back on a client's discount request. But again, if you have to discount to win the business, ask for something in return.

UPSELLING STRATEGY #9

The Eyes Have It

Years ago, I remember deciding that it was time to change to a new cable provider. So I called up the company and scheduled an installation-activation appointment.

The gentleman who arrived, we'll call him Bob, was a true cable installation professional. But more than that, he was the consummate Upseller and he made it seem effortless.

When Bob arrived, he was dressed in the company outfit: logo on his shirt, the company baseball cap, and the fully loaded toolbelt. He was friendly and wasn't afraid to engage in small talk.

Bob asked, "We sure are glad to have you as a new customer. Why did you decide to switch to our company?"

From that statement and question alone, I picked up immediately that Bob was proud of the company he was working with. How did I know this? In two lines Bob made it clear that he was a company man and he had a stake in the company's success. He used the personal pronoun, "*We* sure are..." and a possessive pronoun "...*our* company".

A person only talks like that when they believe in (a) their product or service, and (b) the company that stands behind it. Bob was using the language of pride, something many salespeople

117

need to incorporate into their conversations with customers.

I said, "Sometimes we have poor signal quality or an outage altogether. For what we're paying, we expect more."

"I've heard similar complaints from other customers as well. I think you're going to see a big difference with our service," Bob added.

"That's the hope. I'll be in my office. If you need anything just holler," I responded as I walked away.

About 20 minutes later Bob taps on the door to my office.

"Victor, I'm done, and I just wanted to walk you through the setup and the use of the remote control. Do you have a moment?"

"Of course." I followed Bob to the living room.

He went through the different screens and highlighted some options for a better viewing experience. As he was going through his demo, Bob asked me, "Is that your wife and kids in that picture?"

"Yes."

"I have 3 kids of my own. Ages 4, 9, and 11."

"Mine are 5 and 9."

"Can I show you something?" he asked

I said, "Sure."

"I see that you have the standard package with a limited set of channels. My kids love to watch this particular channel because it has a lot of shows that they love. We also have a craft channel. So if you or your wife are into crafts, you're going to love this. Let me show you."

Bob shows me what's on the craft channel and we both laugh at the thought of me learning how to make a quilt.

"Okay, so maybe you're not a quilt guy. By any chance, do you like sports?

"I like the occasional game of basketball."

"You're a tall guy so you probably played basketball in high school or college."

"Yes, I did." I responded proudly.

"Although this isn't included in your package, we have several sports channels that I think you might like. If you're a March Madness basketball fan, you can watch the games on this channel."

Bob paused to scan a few of the channels so I could see what was on at the moment.

"May I suggest something? You have the standard package, which is really a great starter package at a great price. By moving to the B package, you can have the kid's programming channels and the sports channels for only $10 per month more, which is only an extra $120 per year. That's the cost of taking the family to the movies once. It's a great deal with the only downside being that you'll have to fight your kids for the TV. I can upgrade the package from here if you give me the go ahead."

What was I going to say after that setup and pitch? I simply said, "Sure, why not?"

Upsell complete.

ANATOMY OF AN UPSELL OPPORTUNITY

Upselling is a team sport. Too often we think that ONLY the salesperson is the one who has to do the Upselling. Truth be told, everyone in your company should be an Upseller at a minimum.

If Bob was any other average technician, he would've just done his job, said goodbye, and moved on to the next job. But Bob doesn't see himself as a technician, he sees himself as a contributor to the company as a whole. Again, listen to his language: *we* and *our*. He takes equal ownership in making sure that customers are satisfied.

He dressed like a professional and spoke like a professional, which again is indicative of the pride he takes in his job.

I don't know if Bob was incentivized to Upsell. Maybe he was, maybe he wasn't. It doesn't matter. What does matter is that Bob went beyond his job description. He was selling with passion (I love what my company offers) and purpose (I want you to have the same access I do).

Bob may have been training in how to install and troubleshoot, but I wonder if he was trained on how to Upsell, or did it come naturally from a person who simply believes in the value his company is providing?

UPSELLING IN THE PROCESS

Every sales process has multiple points where an Upselling can be done. For example, let's take Bob's company and let's analyze their sales process.

- (Inbound) I called in and talked to a customer support person

- (Qualify) I was asked a few questions about my current-service and what I wanted

- (Meeting) A meeting is set up for the technician to comeout

- (Installation) Technician installs the service

- (Contract) I sign off on the installation

- (Support) Customer support calls to make sure the installation went well

In this process, there are 3 sales moments with 2 of them being Upsell moments. The first sales moment occurred when I called in and inquired about their services. The support person gave me their pricing and I agreed. A technician (Bob) was then scheduled to come out.

The second sales moment occurred when Bob was in the house. That's the Upsell I've already described where I went from Package A to Package B.

The third sales moment was after the installation, let's say a week later. While I did get a follow-up call to make sure I was satisfied with Bob and the service, the support person didn't try to Upsell me anything else. Some would say another Upsell would be annoying. I would say that's a missed opportunity. Assuming I was extremely happy with their service so far, If the company did have something of even greater value for me, I would've wanted to hear about it.

Every sales process has at least 3 sales moments in them. When there is an agreement, immediately before finalizing the agreement and after (e.g., a week later) the agreement has been signed.

Let me give you one more example regarding Upselling opportunities throughout the sales process. A friend of mine owns a pool company and his sales process is as follows:

- (Inbound) Inbound inquiry by a prospective client

- Qualify) The prospect is qualified over the phone

- (Meeting) A meeting is set up

- (Walk-through) Salesperson joins the prospect at theirhome and they do a walk-through and discuss the possible options

- (Proposal) Salesperson goes back and develops a conceptual design(s) and proposal

- (Meeting) A meeting at the client's home to walk-through the design and options

- (Contract) Contract is signed and an agreed start and-completion date is established

- (Construction): Project manager is assigned, and pool construction begins

- (Completion) A final inspection is made and the customer signs off on the project

- (Follow-up) Salesperson goes back to the client with acelebratory bottle of wine or champagne and addresses lingering concerns, if any.

The first sales moment is when the contract is signed. That's the first agreed upon deal.

The second sales moment occurs during the construction process. This is where the project or construction manager can highlight a few things that may not have been discussed during the proposal phase. For example, the project manager might notice that the pump selected for this particular pool would work more efficiently if a new adapter or configuration were used. It would have to be something that the project manager sees while on location.

The third sales moment happens after the pool is installed and has been used by the customer. The salesperson can visit the customer and during the visit may see a few things that can be done or added to increase the pool's enjoyment. It's worth noting that the third sale could be called the 'pick up' sale, where the salesperson picks up more sales that weren't available or doable during the first sales moment.

Let's go back to the decision fatigue discussion and the patio furniture example. It was only after the pool was complete that the client could focus on buying patio furniture.

How many sales moments are in your process? Of those, how many Upsell moments are there? Few companies actually train salespeople and their support team to Upsell at all times. Imagine the added revenue you or your company could generate with minimal or no added resources by simply focusing on upsell moments. The additional sales are there if we only train ourselves to look for them.

UPSELLING STRATEGY #10

Funnels and Ladders

Over the last few years, the word 'funnel' has come to life in the world of online selling. Most of us are familiar with the word in the context of getting people into the sales funnel using different forms of Inbound or Outbound marketing strategies.

For example, if you go to a trade show in your industry, you'll probably meet a lot of potential buyers or leads who may wind up buying from your company. At this stage of the sales process we say that these new leads we met at the trade show are at the 'top of the funnel' (TOFU is the accepted acronym). That simply means we've met them, but they have yet to be qualified.

The goal then is to reach out to these individuals after the trade show and qualify them by asking a series of questions and having some sort of litmus test to see if they really are potential clients.

During the qualification phase you might use the **BANT** model to qualify the opportunity. **BANT** stands for Budget, Authority, Need, and Timeline. During your lead qualification discussion, you'll find either a circuitous or a direct way to ask if they have a **Budget** or can afford to buy from you. You'll ask questions to discover if they are the **Authority** or decision-maker to ensure you're speaking to the right person. You'll also ask about the current **Need** they have and how your product or service might be able to address them. And lastly, you'll inquire about when they planning on taking action, or what is their **Timeline**. The BANT model is not a sequential qualification tool. By that I mean you don't have to first ask about Budget, then Authority, then Need, and then Timeline. It's a framework or rather a set of boxes that have to be checked to qualify this opportunity before investing more time.

Once qualified, the lead now becomes a prospect (i.e., prospective buyer), and the opportunity is moved into the official sales process. To begin with, you might set up a face-to-face meeting to really dig into the prospect's issue, or simply arrange an online demonstration of your product. Every company has their own process for closing a sale. During the close (proposal and negotiation) phase of the deal, the salesperson may attempt to Upsell the client on other products, as we've already discussed.

Once the deal is closed, the product is delivered and installed with the aim of having a completely satisfied customer. Many companies will follow up with a phone call or send a survey via email to gauge the customer's level of satisfaction. This score is called the Customer Satisfaction (CSAT) score and it's a metric worth tracking along with future Upsell on a per customer basis. In other words, if you have a high CSAT, that should correspond to an increase in customer loyalty and an increase in repeat orders or future business.

Most sales efforts stop here. Once the deal is done and the customer is satisfied, salespeople move on to the next opportunity. Why? It's possible that the salesperson doesn't know where to go from here, what to sell them next. They may not know what type of Upsell will work for that particular customer or situation. Since they don't have a clear path to what to sell next, many just move to another opportunity (i.e., go find new business).

This is where developing value ladders and funnels comes into play.

Up to this point we've only talked about a funnel, singular not plural. The most common funnel is the sales funnel and that's it. But Upselling involves a series of Upsell funnels that move the customer up the value ladder. A value ladder is simply an Upsell to newer products or services that get more expensive as the client moves to the next rung.

Let's look at a typical 'funnels and ladders' configuration or strategy that is often used online. Let's say you're a consulting company who is looking for a specific type of client online. Your service focuses on helping small to medium sized technology companies scale their businesses. Your primary approach for attracting new leads is using Inbound strategies to drive traffic to your website.

The first thing you might do is create a type of bait or piece of content that your ideal client would find desirable. So, you create a white paper or case study on what the best practices are for scaling a business. You promote this case study online by leveraging your social media channels and maybe even some paid advertisement online. The goal of this marketing campaign is to get people (ideal clients) to download the case study for free in exchange for their email address. That's the cost to the person wanting your case study.

Once the email address is captured, the lead (unqualified prospect) will receive an email from your company with instructions on how to download the case study. You are now one rung up on your value ladder.

Let's say you ran this 'free case study' campaign for a month and garnered 200 email addresses. You still don't know who these leads are, so you now want to move them up to the next rung of the value ladder by offering an online assessment of their business for a nominal cost of $100. You send this offer out via email. The hope is that a large percentage of the 200 will buy the online assessment. If they do, they have now qualified themselves to some extent.

Let's assume out of the 200, only 50 decide to do the online assessment. From a revenue standpoint, you've just generated $5,000 (50 potential clients x by $100 assessment fee).

During the online assessment, your company will ask these potential clients for more detailed information about their company and goals in order to provide a helpful assessment along with some recommendations. During the process you'll also collect more information about the person doing the assessment (title, role, responsibilities, phone number, company location and website, etc.).

After the assessment is complete, your company will automatically generate and send an email with the results of the assessment. Another option would be to deliver the results personally over the phone or via video conference or both (email and then call). The end goal is simply to get the lead to review the assessment.

As you're reviewing the assessment, via phone or video conference, your objective is to first provide the lead with valuable insight that was discovered from the online assessment. Your secondary objective is to Upsell the lead into doing an onsite review that will be more thorough and comprehensive (i.e., a deeper dive into the company structure, strategy and finances).

The onsite review is where a representative of your company will go to the client's location and do an exhaustive review. The cost of this review is $10,000. This is the third rung of the value ladder.

Let's suppose that of the 50 who took the online assessment and reviewed the results with you, 20 agree to do an onsite review. Revenue generated at this stage is $200,000 (20 clients multiplied by $10,000 onsite review fee).

After doing an onsite review and providing the client with critical feedback on where they can improve their performance to help scale their business, you offer to develop a training program for their team. The cost of developing and delivering the training is $100,000. This is the fourth rung of the value ladder. Of the 20 who did the onsite review, 5 decide to take you up on developing a customized training program. Revenue generated at this stage is $500,000 (5 clients multiplied by $100,000 for training).

Once the training has been developed and delivered, the salesperson then moves to the next Upsell, which is an annual contract for consultation services that will give a client access to you for the next 12 months, where you will guide them on issues concerning the growth of their business. The annual consulting contract is $360,000 per year. Of the 5 who bought your training and development package, 2 decide to sign a consultation contract. Revenue generated at this stage is $720,000 (2 clients multiplied by $360,000).

Total revenues generated from each stage was:

Stage 1: $0

Stage 2: $10,000

Stage 3: $200,000

Stage 4: $500,000

Stage 5: $720,000

Total revenue generated: $1, 430,000.

It should be emphasized that in this example, Marketing would be responsible for the first stage, getting leads into the funnel by driving traffic to get potential clients to download the case study. Stages 2 through 5 fall into the sales category.

During each of the 4 stages, the salesperson has to develop a compelling sales presentation to move the client up the value ladder. From a selling perspective, the real value of having a value ladder is knowing what is expected of you in the next step. This is important. Many salespeople simply don't know what to Upsell next or don't have a process for it, and therefore leave money on the table.

Study most sales processes today and you'll find that an Upsell process or a follow-up process are usually not part of the sales process or, worse, no one is thinking about Upselling. It doesn't matter if you're an entrepreneur, a small business, or an enterprise company. You can implement a funnel and ladder Upsell process.

UPSELLING STRATEGY #11

Reframing Value

One day my wife and I went to Lowes to pick up some paint for a bathroom project. Before arriving, we had already decided on what color to choose. After looking through the color cards we settled on 'Foggy City', a nice light gray to match our new tiles. We grabbed a can of paint by Brand X and approached the counter to get our paint color matched and mixed. The person behind the counter stepped forward and the following conversation ensued:

Me: "We'd like to have this color and here's the Brand X paint."

Employee: "Great. What are you going to paint?"

Me: "We just remodeled our bathroom so we're looking for a nice color match."

Employee: "You know, for only $2 more you can get Brand Y (another reputable brand) that provides better coverage, it's a much thicker coat that would be better for your bathroom."

(My wife and I both looked at each other as we were caught off guard. It wasn't the $2 that was throwing us. Rather, it was why one quality brand was better than the other.)

Employee: "The brand you're buying is a good brand and would work just fine. On the other hand, Brand Y will give you better coverage and since bathrooms are splash-prone areas that retain moisture, they are also prone to mold and mildew, especially if the bathroom doesn't have good ventilation. Brand Y has anti-microbial additives that resist mold, which will kill existing mold and prevent new mold from growing. And for only $2 more, it's worth it. But it's your call."

Me: (Exchanging a look with my wife again.) "Sure. Why not?"

Employee: "Let me go ahead and get a can of Brand Y, I'll return Brand X to the shelf for you. It'll take about 5 - 10 minutes and I'll place the paint at the end of the counter when it's done in case you have to do any other shopping."

Me: "Thank you."

Let's analyze this simple conversation exchange and transaction. There are a lot of subtle selling techniques embedded.

First, before arriving at the store we knew what brand of paint we wanted to get. Brand X had worked well for us in the past, so we were set on getting that brand. When we walked up to the matching and mixing counter, we were good to go. From an outside perspective we were 100% into the buying cycle: the decision on what brand we were going with was done, what color we had chosen was decided, and we were willing to pay the asking price.

Theoretically, when a customer is this far into the buying cycle, there is nothing that can be done to undo what has already been decided. Think of any past deal you've worked on in B2B or B2C. When the client (customer) makes a definitive decision on the product or service, there's nothing that can be done other than taking the order or running the credit card.

So what happened here? How was the employee able to overturn a buying decision that was supposedly 100% made? This simple exchange highlighted for me that no decision is ever really done. Yes, yes, I concede that some deals might be so far down the track that it might be irreversible. But, until the purchase order is cut, and payment made, assuming no contract has been signed, there's always a small space of time where any decision can be overturned.

When we were at the counter, although we had made our decision, no payment had been made. No final act of commitment had taken place, only in our minds. So although we thought we were 100% into the buying cycle, in hindsight we were at the 99% mark.

Second, we had already sold ourselves on buying the paint. It wasn't a matter of 'if', it was a matter of 'what' when we arrived at the store. In a sense, the first sale was already complete. The $2 Upsell is, in essence, the second sale. Any Upsell is a second sale. The customer decides to make a buying decision and the objective of Upselling is to sell them something that has greater value. Remember, you don't Upsell to sell more, you Upsell to add value to the customer and their buying experience. In the case of the paint, the employee wanted us to have a better quality of paint that would be longer lasting and healthier (no mold).

Third, the employee Upselling us wasn't motivated by a commission. Even if he earned a commission it's not going to be much on a $2 sale. Plus, he seemed really agnostic about the matter, which is a great approach. When you're Upselling a client, it's best to be objective and simply present the facts, which is what he did. His motivation for the Upsell seemed sincere. We truly felt he was giving us a piece of insight to help us make a better decision.

Fourth, customers don't like to feel like they're being pressured into a higher priced purchase, no matter how incremental the difference. When anyone tries to Upsell us it immediately triggers the 'fight - flight' mode in our reptilian primal brain. Humans are wired to protect their resources for survival. Being pressured into paying more is equivalent to someone breaking into our mental cave and taking some of those resources (i.e, money). A $2 Upsell isn't much but it's still enough to trigger the flight or fight mode in our brain. We simply can't help it. The employee, whether he knew it or not, was able to disarm that mode with 2 simple statements: "And for only $2 more, it's worth it. But it's your call." If we were to deconstruct this simple line, we would find that it's loaded with subtle persuasion. Let's take a closer look:

"And, for only $2 more": He was getting us away from focusing on the cost of the cans ($25 vs. $27) and focus on the difference. He was also minimizing the difference ($2) while maximizing the value (last longer, and safer).

"It's worth it": He delivered this statement in a matter-of-fact manner that left no doubt he knew what he was talking about. His tone and body language transmitted that he knew what he was talking about (authority) and that he was giving us, at no cost, the benefit of his expertise.

"But it's your call": By adding this comment, he was emotionally detaching himself from our choice. He was also mentally handing over control and accountability for our decision (i.e., no spending $2 more can cost you in the long run) back to us. When you hand control back to your customer, it's fascinating how much more reflective they become when making a buying decision.

When a salesperson nudges you to make the decision, you

both share in the responsibility. But when a salesperson says "It's your call", we now know that the decision solely lies with us. And, since we hate to make important decisions in isolation, we seek a comrade to share the responsibility. In this case the salesperson. I didn't want it to be my (or my wife's) decision, I wanted it to be our (expert employee, my wife and me) decision.

Fifth, customers aren't always right, but they'd like to be. Customers often do research on an important item before going to the store to purchase it or buying it online. When customers come into your place of business, you should assume they've done some research, or at a minimum have some idea of what they want. The last thing any salesperson wants to do is dismiss what a client knows, and you have to show respect for any decision made. When we approached the counter, the employee didn't say, "Why the heck would you choose this brand?" Even if he were right, that would've been a huge mistake. No customer wants to be made to look stupid. This employee understood and respected the value of the customer's choice by saying, "The brand you're buying is a good brand and would work just fine." With this simple phrase he acknowledged and demonstrated respect for our choice.

Sixth, when you want to get someone to change their mind, you have to follow the request with a solid reason for doing so. Cost saving wouldn't have been enough in this instance, since a $2 saving wouldn't have moved our decision-making needle. Or, imagine if he had said, "This other brand is better and it's only $2 more." The word better is a qualifier, not a quantifier. A qualifier gives you relative information but doesn't quantify the value. You often hear salespeople use phrases like: It's better; It's faster; It's bigger; It's newer.

These qualifiers may give you some relative idea of how their product might compare to someone else's, but it doesn't give you the quantifiable information to back their claim (i.e., it's an opinion, not a fact). If the employee had said, "Brand Y is better than Brand X," this would've triggered the follow-up question, "In what way?"

Saying it's better, faster or cheaper is not a strong sales argument, especially when the item (can of paint) to be purchased is part of a major investment (your house). The company's employee understood that in order to get a consumer to change their mind, you have to give them a compelling reason, beyond price and baseless claims (qualifiers: best, better, cheaper), to do so.

Instead of saying Brand Y is better, he said, "On the other hand, Brand Y will give you better coverage and since bathrooms are splash-prone areas that retain moisture, they are also prone to mold and mildew, especially if the bathroom doesn't have good ventilation. Brand Y has anti-microbial additives that resist mold, which will kill existing mold and prevent new mold from growing."

He was giving us a compelling reason, beyond the $2 difference, to abandon our well thought out choice for a better choice. Read that line again!

When you want to get a customer to switch from one product to another, or from a competitor to you, you have to provide a tangible reason for them to do so. You have to help them make the mental switch by giving them insight to justify the change in their mind or to their management.

And lastly, let's take a closer look at the employee's 'closing statement': "Let me go ahead and get a can of Brand Y, I'll return Brand X to the shelf for you. It'll take about 5 - 10 minutes and I'll place the paint at the end of the counter when it's done in case you have to do any other shopping."

This statement may seem innocuous, but it isn't. For instance, the employee volunteered to walk over and get us the can of paint we decided to go with (Brand Y), and he also volunteered to put Brand X back on the shelf. Why? Because he understood the concept of a frictionless buying experience and how buyers think. When a customer changes his mind, the last thing you want to do is make it hard on them. Instead, make it easy for your customer to change. By offering to return Brand X and retrieve Brand Y he was simplifying the process by reducing the amount of effort, no matter how small, to change. By taking care of the return and retrieval, he was insulating us from changing our minds again:

- By returning Brand X back to the shelf for us he eliminated the possibility of buyer's regret (i.e., I should've gone with the other one).

- By retrieving Brand Y for us, he was eliminating any last-minute doubt and he was also reducing any friction (finding the right shelf and can of paint in the next aisle over).

This simple transaction highlights that selling comes down to what you say, how you say it and when you say it. There are moments in every step of the sales process where how you communicate value can shift the buyer's mindset.

TWO UPSELL SEQUENCES

The key to a good Upsell conversation is the right blend of empathy, authority and detachment.

- Empathy transmits that you care about the customer more than you do about the sale.

- Authority transmits that you have the experience or

knowledge and you want the customer to benefit from that.

- Detachment transmits that whatever the customer decides is fine with you.

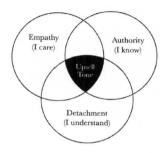

If you analyze the $2 Upsell conversation, you'll find that the employee had this blend in how he communicated the value of the product. Here's one more example on how to shift the buyer's preference and Upsell them on a more valuable product.

Let's go back to the paint section. Imagine for a moment that you walk into a store to buy a can of paint. You're confronted with two choices: Brand X, which cost $15, and Brand Y, which cost $20. As you mull it over you rationalize to yourself that both cans are apparently of equal value and you decide to go with the least expensive one. Recall that when the brain is facing uncertainty it will react by mitigating risk. In this case, better to go with the cheaper one than the more expensive one.

At that precise moment, a store assistant walks by and notices you mulling over the decision and says,

"You know, I strongly recommend Brand X. It's a higher price but it will last 8 years and provide better coverage where Brand Y will only last 4 years. That means that over 8 years you'd have to buy Brand X twice, which will cost you $30. So in reality, Brand Y costs less and you only have to paint once instead of twice."

Now let's stop here and analyze this conversation. The buyer has already made a mental decision to go with the cheaper brand. The store assistant then interrupts the buying cycle before any financial commitment (i.e., payment) has been made. Remember, there's a transactional gap between the decision to buy something and actually paying for it. So although the mental decision to buy was made (i.e., first sale), there's still time to get the Upsell (i.e., second sale).

The buyer at this point has now been given new information to consider, a couple of reasons for paying more for a superior product:

1. Brand Y is more expensive, but it will last longer, and,

2. Provide better coverage over Brand X.

One would think at this point the Upsell has been made. But not so fast. Sometimes the reason we provide a client to induce them to buy may seem sufficient from our point of view, but not sufficient from theirs. Their priorities for wanting to save money may not align with your rationale for a higher priced item. For example, the customer may say something like this:

Customer: "Well, I'm preparing to sell my home so I don't care how long the paint will last."

The salesperson now realizes that it's not about the quality of the paint that matters to the customer. So, the salesperson needs to demonstrate empathy and understand the customer's real motive(s).

Salesperson: "I understand, but I still think Can B is the better choice. You see, Can B contains 50% more pigment, which results in better coverage than Can A. This means you will need to apply only one coat. If you have a dark wall, you'll have to apply 2 coats with Can A, which will double your labor and your cost."

Client: "Hmm ..."

Salesperson: "Plus, you are guaranteed that your house will look freshly painted, which in turn improves your chances of selling your home. Can you see how spending an additional $5 is a great investment to sell your home at the price you want."

Client: "I see your point."

This is a perfect example of how a salesperson has to align their value proposition with the customer's real motivations. Demonstrating empathy, authority and detachment will allow you to Upsell more effectively.

UPSELLING STRATEGY #12

Utilization Rate

Utilization and Life Cycle are important concepts to keep in mind when attempting to Upsell a customer. Utilization is the principle of usage; how many times will I use an item? Life Cycle is the number of times or time periods you will use the item.

For example, let's say you decide you want to buy a high-end camera and the price is $5,000. If you're a novice and aren't quite sure you'll be taking that many photos, then you're not likely to buy it. If you estimate that you'll use the camera once a month (12 times a year) at most, you'll instinctively find the camera price too high. In this case, to calculate Utilization you would use the following formula:

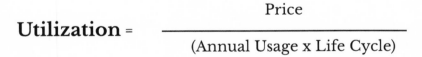

$$\textbf{Utilization} = \frac{\text{Price}}{(\text{Annual Usage x Life Cycle})}$$

Price = Price you pay for the item

Annual Usage = How many times you'll use the item in 12 months

Life Cycle = How many years you plan to own the item

To calculate the customer Utilization Rate of the camera would be:

Utilization = ($5,000) / (12 times X 1 year) = **$416.67**

That means that the consumer will be paying $416.67 every time they use the camera in the first year alone. If they estimate that they would own and use the camera for 2 years, then the Utilization Rate would be half that.

Utilization = $5000) / (12 x 2) = **$208.34**

This number might still be too high for an average consumer to justify the purchase. Granted, most consumers won't actually do the calculation when they're buying the camera, but they can intuit rather quickly that paying $5,000 is way too much for what they want to do.

A professional photographer who makes their living shooting photos will have a lower Utilization cost. The photographer estimates that they will use the camera 2-3 times per week or an average of 10 times per month (120 times per year). This photographer also knows that lens technology changes greatly and that buying a camera every two years (i.e., Life Cycle) is a good idea.

Utilization = $5,000 / (120 x 2) = **$20.83**

A Utilization Rate of $20.83 might seem like a lot to an average consumer, but to a professional photographer who charges, let's say, $500 per shooting session, this is just a minor cost of doing business.

Utilization is a very useful tool for Upselling a customer. It serves as a justification by helping the customer rationalize why the purchase makes sense, and it has the effect of shifting the focus from what you're paying (price) to what it's really costing you.

Gym memberships are prime examples of how salespeople use Utilization Rates. If a local fitness center charges $99 per month, a customer might initially think that the price seems a bit high. The salesperson at the gym then says something like, "The average member uses the gym 4 times a week, which is about 16 times a month, which comes to a little over $6 a visit.

Monthly Utilization = ($99) / (16 times x 1 month) = **$6.19**

This is an instance where calculating the Life Cycle on a monthly basis, instead of yearly, is more impactful. It should be noted that the Utilization Rate is the same whether you calculate it annually or monthly.

Annual Utilization = ($99 x 12 months) / ((16 times x 12 months) x (1 year)) =
$1188 / 192 times x 1 year = $6.19

Selling a customer on $99 per month is easier than selling an annual contract at $1,118. The former seems like a smaller commitment, even though the Utilization Rates are the same

Fitness centers are notorious for breaking down Utilization Rates even further. It's a strategy called 'reducing to the ridiculous'. The premise is you keep breaking down or reducing the Utilization Rate so low that buying the item seems like a no-brainer.

"The average member uses the gym 4 times a week, which is about 16 times a month, which comes to a little over $6 a visit. And, If you spend 2 hours on average working out, that means you're essentially paying $3 an hour ($6 a visit divided by 2 hours) to access all our exercise equipment and amenities, which include the pool, steamrolls and saunas. Can you see how

$99/month really isn't that expensive?"

The majority of customers don't think in terms of Utilization because:

1. They're programmed to focus on price

2. They undervalue (or underestimate) how often they usethe item

3. They're thinking short-term, not long-term

By using a Utilization Rate, you can again shift the customer's attention away from price towards that of value (i.e., how much usage they'll derive from buying the item). By giving them a Life Cycle to consider (i.e., number of years they'll enjoy the benefits of the item), you're reframing how they evaluate the value by stretching their value timeline.

One last example, pool companies. Pool companies have discovered another way of using Utilization and Life Cycle to sell to customers. Instead of selling to you on usage (the number of times you'll use it), they'll instead sell to you on what it will cost to own your own. If, for example, a newly constructed pool price was $85,000, the price alone might be a deterrent for the average middle-class buyer. But pool salespeople are quick to remind customers that a fiberglass pool has a 25-year Life Cycle.

Annual Utilization: ($85,000) / (25 years) = **$3,400**

A salesperson might pitch the usage value this way: "How much is it worth to you to have your own private pool to use whenever you want, free of strangers and annoyances? Is that worth $3,400 a year?"

If you want to 'reduce it to the ridiculous', you would say, "The average family uses the pool about 150 times per year. That means you get to enjoy your pool for about $23 ($3,400 /

150 times) every time your family uses it. And, if it's a family of 4, that's less than $6 per person. That's cheaper than a movie and the memories you'll have ... invaluable!"

Whether or not you agree with this approach, the fact remains that Utilization can help you shift customers away from the price and get them to focus on the value your product delivers in the long-run.

Now, you may be thinking, "There's no way I could justify buying a pool with a 25-year timeline! What if I decide to move after 10 years?"

A shorter timeline means you simply have to create more value for the buyer in a shorter period of time. Instead of a Utilization Rate of $3,400, you now have to sell them on a Utilization of $8,500 cost per year ($85,000 / 10 years).

Annual Utilization: ($85,000) / (150 times x 10 years) = **$56.67**

"The average family uses the pool about 150 times per year. That means you get to enjoy your pool for about $56 every time your family uses it. And, if it's a family of 4, that's less than $14 per person. That's cheaper than a movie (with popcorn and drinks), without having to leave your home. And, the memories you'll have ... invaluable!"

In this over simplified example, by adding the popcorn and drinks I'm creating more value as a counter lever to the $14 per person. The key here is that the customer may not have considered the full price of a movie experience (e.g., ticket price + popcorn + drinks + travel time to and from the theatre). By highlighting these amenities, you are reframing (or reshaping) the customer's perception of the value of owning a pool.

In a SaaS (software as a service) enterprise environment,

your client may be solely focused on how much they will have to pay per user to access a productivity software. A 100-person company may have to pay $50,000 per year to access the software which might seem high to the client. You can reduce this to the ridiculous by pointing out that access to the software will be $500 per person per year and if we take into account that the average number of working days in a year is 261 day, that means that each person is paying $1.92 per day to access data across a number of projects and clients.

So whether you're selling B2B or B2C, the Utilization strategy can help the buyer justify paying more now for long-term benefit(s). In an Upsell scenario, adding more products to the original order and amortizing it (i.e., averaging the cost over time), makes it more palatable for the buyer and allows you to increase the average order size.

UPSELLING STRATEGY #13

Make it a Process

As salespeople and as a company, the need to have an Upselling process as part of the overall sales strategy is imperative. Every day that goes by is another day where money was literally left on the table.

Upselling and its variants (i.e., add-ons, bundling, Cross-Sell) are less likely to be implemented in the real world because we simply don't make it part of our sales DNA. Sales training courses are quick to teach you about strategies, tactics and processes, but you'll find scant messaging on the power of Upselling. That needs to change. We need to have a more forceful discussion on how Upselling can help and find a way to institutionalize it until it becomes a sales habit.

As I mentioned earlier, existing clients are more likely to buy from you, be more loyal and stick around longer, as long as you are providing them continuous or dependable value. Studies attribute up to 35% of additional sales to the use of Upselling strategies. If this is indeed the case, then why is it that we keep ignoring it or resisting its importance?

Many executives and managers know that Upselling is important and can contribute significantly to the bottom line, yet no formal processes are put in place. I strongly believe it's because a company is unable to quantify its value, more specifically a customer's Lifetime Value (LTV). Companies generate a lot of data like:revenue by quarter, revenue by customer, customer retention rates or churn rates, etc. But what I rarely see is a number for quantifying the LTV of a client.

Imagine a monthly metric whereby each customer is scored not only on what they've purchased, but on what the potential purchasing power is over the next year or two. Further imagine if each customer had a potential revenue score attached to them; like a credit card score that tells you their LTV potential. Salespeople would then be able to shift their attention away from closing any deal to a longer time horizon based on LTV.

In other words, aggregating and analyzing customer data allows companies to be able to score customers not solely in terms of how much they've purchased, but how much they would expect to buy over the coming years. Imagine combing your data to score a client before they purchased anything in terms of long-term potential. With data analytics and artificial intelligence, this is now possible. For example, let's say you have two companies:

- Company A has $50M in annual revenue, has been around 10 years, has 100 employees, and a list of other data points. You currently have a proposal on the table for $250,000.
- Company B has $10M in revenue, has been in business 2 years, has 15 employees and a list of other data points.You currently have a proposal on the table for $100,000.

Where should you focus your attention? Well, if you're a short-term thinker with short-term goals, then obviously Company A wins this bake-off. But, what if we go back into our client history and find similar client types and analyze their behavior after the initial purchase? What if the existing customer data from in your system could tell you (i.e., predict) how loyal a customer type would be (i.e., how many years will they continue to buy from you) and how much each customer would spend during their lifetime? The investigation into the data might find that companies with a Company A type of profile will buy for only 3 years, whereas companies like Company B types will buy for 5 years. The data may look something like this:

Company A

Year 1: $250,000

Year 2: $50,000

Year 3: $25,000

Company B:

Year 1: $100,000

Year 2: $150,000

Year 3: $100,000

Year 4: $50,000

Year 5: $50,000

What this type of data would tell us, from an Upselling perspective, is that Company B is a much better (i.e., highly valued) client over the long run. Having this data would guide the salesperson to shift his focus from short- to long-term, prioritize Company B over Company A and give him the confidence to pursue Upselling opportunities after the initial sale.

Think about it for a minute. If a salesperson knew, based on historical data that a company would be willing to spend more over time, how would their sales approach change?

- Would they be more focused (keep the company at the top of the sales stack)?

- Would they be more inquisitive (dig deeper for other opportunities)?

- Would they be more aggressive (have the confidence topursue other opportunities within the company)?

- The answer to all three questions is a strong "Yes".

THE PROBLEM

Why aren't more companies looking at their existing customer base for new (Cross-Sell) or more (Upsell) business? More to the point, why are salespeople not being more inclusive in their sales strategy when it comes to incorporating an Upsell process?

UNAWARE Didn't consider upselling options.	UNWILLING Are afraid to go back to customer for fear of distabiliztion or lack of satisfaction.
UNPREPARED Don't know how to approach an existing client or has no process for it.	UNCONVINCED Don't believe uselling works or worth the ROI.

The answer might lie in one of these four quadrants:

- **Unaware:** As hard as it may be to believe, some salespeople never even consider Upselling as an option to increase their sales revenue. It's simply not top-of-mind. This type of salesperson is focused on closing new deals. Like a horse with blinders, it only sees the immediate opportunity.

- **Unprepared:** Some salespeople don't know how to go about Upselling. As we've discussed in this book, there are many ways to approach Upselling. Salespeople are taught the fundamentals: closing, prospecting, sales process, asking the right questions, listening skills, demonstrating, and presenting. When Upselling is indeed covered during the training program, it's as an afterthought or something to consider. Worse still, they see no strong connection on how using Upselling can help them achieve their revenue goal so they aren't motivated to learn how.

- **Unwilling:** Salespeople may not want to go back to talk to a client because they have an imagined fear that the client might be offended or feel taken advantage of. If you're honestly offering real value on the Upsell, there is nothing to fear. Yet many salespeople are unwilling to go back to a client because they're afraid it might open up a can of worms (i.e., the client isn't happy with what they purchased). To be fair, in some marginal cases, their unwillingness may be a symptom of the company not delivering on its value promise.

- **Unconvinced:** There are salespeople who have done some sort of cost benefit analysis and concluded that going back to Upsell existing clients is not worth the time or effort compared to finding new clients. They'd rather work on finding bigger deals and not spend their time selling add-ons.

IMAGINED FEAR

The unwillingness to sell to existing clients may be driven

by fear, an imagined fear but fear nonetheless. An imagined fear is a fear you've conjured up in your mind that has nothing to do with reality.

For those salespeople in the Unwilling Quadrant, let's analyze their 2 biggest fears: "Don't mess with a good thing!" and "What if I go back and they're not happy?"

1) Don't Mess With a Good Thing!: This is the fear that trying to sell more to their existing clients might somehow upset the proverbial apple cart. Trying to sell more (Upsell) or something else (Cross-Sell) might jeopardize the existing business relationship (i.e., guaranteed future sales or ability to get referrals).

When I was a B2B salesman, I remember some of our clients were on open purchase orders. That meant that the client could directly order products against a pre-approved purchase order without a salesperson needing to intervene. The purchase order was often times sent into purchasing and processed without the salesperson even being aware that the order was placed. A deal like this was easy commissions for a salesperson. So easy that once it was set up, they never attempted to go back and Upsell to a client on our newer products. Did the thought occur to them to go back and try to add more products to the open purchase order? I'm sure it did. And I'm also sure their thinking was, "Don't mess with a good thing!"

2) What if they're not happy?: Another fear of approaching an existing client might be the discovery of their sense of unhappiness or discontent with your product or service. Salespeople fear going back to an existing account because they don't want to hear bad news. The client might not be happy with the product or they simply don't believe your product met their expectations.

I offer the following as a personal example. A few years ago, my friend Hal told me about a guy named Mike who knew a lot about video equipment. I agreed to go with Hal over to Mike's house for advice. By the end of the 3-hour session, Mike has sold me on $2,000-worth of equipment. Hal and I loaded up the car and home I went to create video courses. Mike and I never talked after that until a few years later. Mike remembered me and immediately started apologizing, in his polite way, saying things like, "Well I hope you didn't think I was pressuring you that day," and "My intention wasn't to have you come over so I can sell you." He repeatedly kept finding opportunities to clarify if not justify the sale he made me years ago.

I finally said, "Mike, that day changed my life." He looked perplexed. I continued, "That was the day I made a decision to build my business using video marketing. I couldn't be happier with that purchase. Best investment in my business to date. For that I want to thank you."

Mike was stunned. Why? Mike's problem was that he took away a totally different impression from that transaction. He thought he was pressuring me to buy something I didn't want. Wrong! In reality, he gave me the kick up the backside and the tools I needed to get started.

Now, what if Mike would've followed up with me to find out how things were going? He might've discovered how content I was. Do you think he could've sold me more? Absolutely! Instead, his imagined fear prevented him from doing so. His imagined fear cost him business and it probably cost me as well. How? If Mike had sold me more equipment (tools), could I have been more effective at producing better content? And would that better content have generated me more business? I guess we'll never know.

Lastly, there is opportunity in dissatisfaction. If the client is indeed unhappy, now's the time to come in and be the hero instead of letting a company complain, affecting your Customer Satisfaction (CSAT) or Net Promoter Score (NPS). It's also an opportunity to learn and turn it around.

Never hide from your clients. When you show up when things are bad, and you turn it around and deliver on the original promise, a real relationship is formed. A loyal client is born.

BEST PRACTICES

1. Incorporate Upselling and its variants (Cross-Sell, Add-On-Sales, Bundling) as part of your sales training program. A good start would be to incorporate the relevant lessons inthis book.

2. Teach your sales team how to value-condition the prospectfor an Upsell by mentioning other available options throughout their sales process, more specifically their sales presentation or demonstrations.

3. Determine in your sales process where Upselling happens. There are three options:

- **Option 1:** Should the Upsell attempt be in the pricingproposal (e.g., 3 options, Good-Better-Best)?

- **Option 2:** Should it happen post-agreement or pre-purchase? For example, the client has decided on purchasing but has not paid for it with a credit card (B2C scenario),or has not signed the contract, or approved the purchaseorder (B2B scenario).

- **Option 3:** Should it happen post-purchase? You followup with a client after a predetermined period of time.

4. Create a value ladder or Upsell Matrix. Salespeople need guidance when it comes to what to Upsell and in what sequence. We've already discussed Value Ladders, now let's consider an Upsell Cross Matrix. A Value Ladder is organized around a sequence: what to sell next in a linear fashion. A matrix offers you flexibility in what to sell and how to sell it (See figure).

Product Sold	Upsell Options	Special Instructions
Product #1	Item A Item B Item C	Value Propsition: (Description) Potential Objections: (Rebuttals)
Product #2	Item D Item E Item F	Value Propsition: (Description) Potential Objections: (Rebuttals)
Product #3	Item D Item E Item F	Value Propsition: (Description) Potential Objections: (Rebuttals)

For example, if you sold Product 1 to a client, then there are 3 different Upsells (Item A, B and C) you can approach the client with. Having this tool available for salespeople is vitally important. Remember, the goal is to always reduce the friction in the sales process. When a salesperson doesn't have to think about what to Upsell and uses the matrix as a map, it makes Upselling that much more understandable, less intimidating and easier.

Another way to use the matrix is as a sales training tool for conditioning your prospect. If the salesperson is selling Product 1 and knows, based on the Matrix, that items A, B and C will be Upsell options, he can begin to mention those items (i.e., condition the client by making them aware of options) during the sales presentations or throughout the sales process.

5. Qualify Post Sale: Learn to qualify clients for future Upselling opportunities. Every CRM should have a field(s) for Upselling potential. When a sale is made, the salesperson should be able to score the client on the probability of an Upsell and what specific items should be offered in the Up sell.

For example, if the client buys Product 2 from the matrix, the salesperson should enter a probability score for an Upsell and which of the 3 items (D, E or F) should be offered during the Upsell opportunity (attempt). A value can then be attached to those opportunities based on the price of the item and quantity. From this, salespeople and managers can run end-of-month reports to see where revenue opportunities might be found. This report will also be useful during lulls in the salesperson's schedule or if there's a shortfall between the revenue goal and opportunities in the pipeline.

6. Create a schedule of calls to Upsell opportunities. Allhabits are formed by first identifying what it is you wantto improve and then make 'When- Then' decision rules.

For example, let's say you do consider Upselling important and you do consider it a priority, but the day seems to get away from you and you end up not making any follow-up calls to existing clients. To make it a habit, create a THEN-WHEN rule(s).

- **Rule #1:** WHEN I'm done with my Monday morning meeting, I will THEN take 10 minutes to write down 5existing clients I will call this week.

- **Rule #2:** Each day, WHEN 3 p.m. rolls around, THEN I will call at least 1 existing client to check in on how things are going, what else they might need, and send a proposal.

Here are some good Upsell questions to ask during an Upsell call:

- What's your vision (or revenue goal) for the next year?

- As you grow, where do you see some needs arising?

- Based on the equipment/supplies you have today, will that be enough to fulfill the demand as you grow?

These questions condition the client to think about the future and their needs. Your job is to tie those future needs to your product or service.

Incorporating an Upselling strategy as part of your sales process begins with awareness (i.e., what do I need to do) and ends with commitment (i.e., when-then rules). Creating simple rules will eventually become part of your routine (i.e., a habit); that's the end goal. When Upselling becomes a primary habit, not an ancillary task, you'll find yourself picking up more unexpected business.

7. Develop Upselling Metrics. The only way to measure success is to measure how much clients are buying, and howoften. A good strategy for this is the RFM model, which isused for analyzing customer value. RFM stands for:

- Recency – How recently did the customer purchase(B2C scenario) or the average deal size (B2B scenario)?

- Frequency – How often do they purchase?

- Monetary Value – How much do they spend or purchase order size?

When it comes to Upselling, bundling is an important strategy, so I would add 2 other metrics to consider:

- Number of SKUs (Stock Keeping Units) per order.

156

Thenumber of SKUs is a good measure of how many additional items are being added to the first sale

- Gross Profit Margin (GPM) is a good metric for monitoring price points (discounts) being offered in packaged deals (i.e., bundles)

Making Upselling part of your sales process and monitoring key metrics for results is a winning combination. If the metrics are falling short or declining, then there must be something that needs fixing in the sales (Upsell) process.

UPSELLING STRATEGY #14

Phrases +Why

Asking someone to consider buying more still leaves the buyer asking themselves the question "Do I really need it?" or "Does it make sense?" Sometimes an Upsell feature might be apparent, in which case it makes sense to buy. In most cases, the buyer is trying to rationalize (make sense of it) and/or justify (will I utilize it enough?) the Upsell. Our job as salespeople is to help clients make that buying decision by giving them a reason(s) to do so (i.e., Here's why you should).

The challenge, though, is finding a way to initiate an Upsell conversation without being seen as overzealous and make it part of the natural flow of the conversation.

With this in mind, below you'll find a list of Upsell phrases you can use to initiate an Upsell conversation while still sounding natural. Each phrase is meant to get the customer to consider buying more of something (Upsell) or additional add-ons (Cross-Sell). Each phrase may also be accompanied with a reason as to why they should buy more to help them justify the added expense.

Formula: Upsell Phrase + Why Buy = **Upsell**

UPSELL PHRASE #1: "WILL THAT BE ENOUGH?"

Customers hate to be caught short or wanting. They resent being limited. Therefore, you can exploit this negative reactance by making them aware in the moment that what they're buying might be limited (i.e., not enough). For example, a person who is buying a computer with a given processor and hard drive size may be content with their choice. To get them to consider upgrading processing speed and/or hard drive capacity, you can simply say, "Based on what you told me and how you'll be using it, will XX memory be enough? Here's why I'm asking. If you're going to ... then ..." This strategy assumes that you've asked the customer enough questions about why they're buying a new computer and how they will use it. This will allow you to formulate a strong 'why buy' statement.

UPSELL PHRASE #2: "BY THE WAY ..."

One of my favorite ways to initiate an Upsell conversation naturally is to insert a (not so) random thought into the conversation using "By the way" (BTW). Let's say you're talking to a customer and you see an opportunity to mention something else they might be interested in. You can casually say, "By the way, the computer that you're buying does come with a [fill in the blank], but you'll also need to consider [fill in the blank]. Here's why I think that's important."

Take a moment to consider your sales process, more specifically the proposal phrase where the customer has begun to narrow down their choices and may be having some difficulty in deciding. A BTW statement can also be used to help guide the customer in making a decision. Think of it as a mental nudge along the decision-making path. The customer is considering, let's say, 2 options and may be paralyzed by buyer's regret (i.e., making the wrong choice). By inserting a BTW statement at the right moment would prevent that from happening. For example,

"By the way, Bill, both of these options are good. You can't go wrong. I would recommend you consider Option B, albeit a bit more expensive, but here's why it'll be worth it in the long run."

UPSELL PHRASE #3: "NOW THAT YOU MENTIONED THAT ..."

Being good at Upselling requires that you listen carefully to what the customer is saying and be in constant surveillance mode for any visual cues as to what else the customer might be interested in. During a conversation with a customer, the customer may say something, or you see something that triggers you to consider adding something to the sales conversation. "Bill, now that you mentioned that, let me show you what I would add if I were you and why." This Upsell phrase is powerful because it's using something the customer said to trigger the Upsell conversation, but it could also be triggered by something you saw.

Let's consider a B2C scenario where a customer is trying to decide between 2 high-end cooking grills for their new backyard. You notice (see) the customer leaning in and taking a closer look at the construction of one of the grills. You can say, "I see that you're looking at the construction of the base. Let me show you what this one has over the other and why it's important."

UPSELL PHRASE #4: "EARLIER ON I TOLD YOU ABOUT ..."

The phrase is a great 'call back' to a previous anchor you dropped. You may have mentioned a particular option early on in the sales or buying process. You then harken back (i.e., call back) to the statement or product you demonstrated. For example, "Jane, earlier on I told you about how our enterprise platform will allow you to track usage and generate utilization reports. Here's why you might want to consider adding this option to your dashboard."

You'll note in this example I used the word 'might' as opposed to the word 'should'. Both are okay. The word 'should' has a more forceful meaning than the word 'might'. I highlight this because it's important to keep in mind that words have force behind them. It's up to you to choose which one fits your style of selling. There is no right or wrong, it's all context. Some clients don't like to be pressured, so 'might' may be appropriate. Other clients need a nudge, so 'should' might work better. It's your call. Besides 'might', other ventilating modifiers you can use to soften the Upsell pitch are 'may' or 'could'.

Example #1: "You may want to consider the following, and here's why." A more forceful way would be "You should consider the following, and here's why."

Example #2: In this statement, I used 2 ventilating modifiers, "You could go ahead and add [insert here], and here's why it might be a good idea." A more forceful approach sans modifiers would be, "You would need to go ahead and add [insert here], and here's why."

UPSELL PHRASE #5: "IF I WERE YOU …" OR "IF IT WERE MINE TO DO …"

Everyone wants inside information, or at least feel that they're getting information no one else has. Buyers are often times overwhelmed by the number of choices and options, which can lead to a no-decision outcome. Not good. We also know that buyers want your advice; what would you do if you were in their situation? If you've positioned yourself as a domain expert, they want to know what you would do. "Look, if it were me, here's what I would do and why." The more personal you can make the experience of using or consuming the product (service) the more impactful your Upsell pitch will be.

In this scenario it's worth noting that adding a ventilating modifier (might, could, may) undermines your authority posture and, therefore, your chances of nudging the customer forward. As an expert, customers don't want any 'wishy washy' statement like, "Look, if it were me here's what I might do." When using either of these authoritative Upsell phrases ("If I were you" or "If it were mine to do"), I would caution against any wording that makes you sound unsure.

UPSELL PHRASE #6: "IF YOU'RE GOING TO ..."

Using this phrase is ideal when a customer is considering buying a specific product and has pretty much committed and is ready to execute the purchase. In the back of your mind the sale is done, but you could offer them something better. "If you're going to [fill in the blank], you might as well [fill in the blank]. Here's why ..." Go back to my can of paint example where the person behind the counter Upsold me on a can of paint that was $2 more.

UPSELL PHRASE #7: "YOU MENTIONED EARLIER THAT ..."

As we've already discussed, listening to your customer is key when it comes to Upselling. Listen for those little things that will help you later on in the sales presentation process. You can then say, "You mentioned earlier that you do a lot of presentations. Let me show you what we have that will work well and why it will enhance your presentations." The customer will appreciate that (a) you were actually listening to them, and (b) you also come across as earnest, making the sale that much more engaging and believable.

UPSELL PHRASE #8: "HERE ARE A FEW OPTIONS TO CONSIDER."

Sometimes you'll come across buyers who already know what they want. They're 80% into the buying cycle and simply need a nudge to buy. When you have this type of customer, you can guide them to what they already know and maybe even add an additional item they haven't considered. In this case the customer says they're interested in a particular item or solution. You kick off the conversation with, "Well, here are a few options to consider ..." (Note: This might be the only exception where a 'why' declaration isn't needed, since the conversation itself is still in the exploratory phase. If you choose to add the why, here's one suggestion: "Well, here are a few options to consider, and here's why.")

UPSELL PHRASE #9: "WHAT I FIND REALLY USEFUL IS ..."

Customers want your opinion, especially if you are perceived as an expert in that domain. Let's say you're selling a SaaS (software as a service) product that has 3-tiers of service. You mention the 3-tiers of pricing and quickly move into the differentiating features of each tier. You then mention a feature and add, "What I find really useful is [fill in the blank], and here's why." This is a perfect way of inserting something you really care about and something that the client may not have thought of.

UPSELL PHRASE #10: "IF YOU'RE JUST GETTING STARTED, HERE'S WHAT I WOULD DO." (VARIATION: WHEN I STARTED OUT, HERE'S WHAT I DID.)

Buyers who are just getting started are afraid of over-buying but they're also afraid of not buying enough. They're looking for the Goldilocks answer: Too hot, too cold ... ah ... just right. This again is another opportunity to position yourself as the expert and provide expert opinion. "Bill, if you're just getting started, here's what I would do and here's why." You can modify this statement a bit by empathizing with them (i.e., letting them

163

know that you understand their dilemma). "Look, if you're just getting started, you don't want to pay too much but you also don't want to get caught not having enough. So here's what I would do, and here's why."

UPSELL PHRASE #11: "HAVE YOU THOUGHT ABOUT [SOMETHING INTRIGUING AND RELEVANT]?" (VARIATION: "HAVE YOU EVER THOUGHT ABOUT ...?")

This is where you, the seller, maintain a macro view of the customer micro conversation. In other words, sometimes the buyer is deep into the details or minutiae that they don't see the bigger picture or are simply missing a vital perspective. "Have you thought about [something intriguing and relevant]?" is a great question to ask to 'interrupt' a buyer's thought process, and it puts them on a different thought track. For example, if the buyer is focused on how his applications will run on his computer given the storage capacity, you can interrupt his thought pattern by asking, "Have you thought about using an external drive or moving all your least used applications (and associated files) to the cloud?" The Upsell here would be an external drive or a cloud subscription. If the buyer says no they haven't considered that, you then reply, "Here's why you should consider it and here are some of the immediate benefits. [Explain.]" (Note: You can use the preamble question, "Let me ask you a question. Have you thought about [fill in the blank]? But be careful. Asking someone, "Can I ask you a question?" might come across as too 'sales-y'. Watch your tone and approach to execute it without triggering sales reactance.

UPSELL PHRASE #12: "DID YOU KNOW ...?"

A great way to grab a customer's attention is to ask an

164

intriguing question. "Did you know that you could ...?" This question is a pattern-interrupt because it's unexpected and intriguing at the same time. The customer might respond with a no. You then respond with, "Here's why it's important and worth your consideration. [Explain.]"

The 'Did you know' (DYK) phrase is especially effective at delivering customer insights. I define insight as information beyond the obvious. A DYK opener can also be used to shift a buyer's attention to a specific detail they may not have considered. "Did you know that by moving your applications to the cloud, you'll be able to [insert details here]. Here's why that matters. [Insert explanation.]"

UPSELL PHRASE #13: "HOW OFTEN DO YOU [FILL IN THE BLANK]?" + "HERE'S WHY I'M ASKING."

This phrase is another pattern-interrupt. A customer might be focused on the immediate needs and may be discounting how often or to what extent they'll utilize the product. For example, you ask, "How often do you (travel)?"

Customer, "Twice a month."

You reply, "Here's why I'm asking."

You can add the 'Did you know' phrase to give the answer more depth. "Here's why I'm asking. Did you know that when you travel twice a month you need to be able to [fill in the blank] and you also need a [fill in the blank]?"

Customer responds with either a surprised look or a statement "I never thought of that."

You've just given the customer some insight and positioned yourself as a source of great information and knowledge.

165

UPSELL PHRASE #14: "SOMETHING MOST PEOPLE NEVER CONSIDER IS ..."

The role of every salesperson is to help, in earnest, customers make the right decision for the right need. Sometimes customers are unaware of what they need or simply haven't considered a particular need. This is where you step in and say, "Something most people never consider is [fill in the blank]. Again, you're providing insight, a considered perspective. And then add, "And here's why it matters." (Variation: "And here's why it's a mistake.") This type of insight builds a quick bond between you, the seller, and the buyer. Buyers are risk averse, so anything you can tell them to help them avoid making a mistake in judgement will endear you to them.

UPSELL PHRASE #15: "HERE'S SOMETHING YOU SHOULD SERIOUSLY CONSIDER."

Again, customers are looking for guidance. They're overwhelmed by all the choices available to them. So overwhelmed that they often overlook the obvious or minimize something you consider extremely important. When you say, "Something you should seriously consider is [fill in the blank], and here's why." The word 'should' is not a suggestion as much as it is a directive or a command. Adding the word 'seriously' gives the statement more weight and significance. These 2 words combined, should and seriously, will trigger the buyer's primal brain into paying attention.

UPSELL PHRASE #16: "WHEN I STARTED OUT, I USED [FILL IN THE BLANK], BUT I SOON REALIZED [FILL IN THE BLANK]."

Customers want to talk to someone who is human and fallible, just like them. They also want to benefit from your experience, not make the same mistakes you made. Which is why using the statement "When I started out ..." is a confession of the sort. You're telling your customer that you thought one way, but when you got knee-deep into it you realized you needed to do it another way. Sharing this type of personal experience is powerful. It lets the customer know that you are a 'product of the product' (i.e., you not only sell it, you've used it and have benefit from it). This perspective helps the customer avoid making a similar mistake, lowers their anxiety, and generates a sense of gratitude (i.e., thank you so much for being open and honest about your experience with the product).

UPSELL PHRASE #17: "LET ME SHOW YOU SOMETHING THAT'S REALLY COOL."

This is a fun phrase that will pique anyone's interest. You will literally see a customer perk up when you use this phrase. Why? Because we all want to see something 'cool'. That said, make sure that whatever you share or demonstrate really has a high cool factor. "Let me show you something that's really cool." Showing and then telling them why, beyond being cool, will help (benefit) them.

UPSELL PHRASE #18: "HERE'S HOW OTHER CUSTOMERS ARE USING X." OR "HERE'S WHAT OTHER CUSTOMERS ARE FINDING."

Customers don't want to feel alone when making a decision. When we don't know what to do (or buy), we immediately search our environment for social proof (i.e., what others are doing or saying). For example, when you go on Amazon.com to buy a product, one of the first things I'm sure you do is look at how

167

many stars the product has gotten and the number of reviews. You'll then proceed to read the negative reviews first and then move on to the positive. The hope during our search, if we like the product, is that the positive reviews will far outweigh the negative ones. In a face-to-face situation, reading reviews may not be possible, so the next best thing is to tell the customer what other customers like them have done (chosen) and why. For example, "Jill, here's what other customers are saying about the product and why they like it." Or, you can make it more relatable by sharing a similar customer or company situation. "One of my customers who runs a business similar to yours purchased this product about a month ago. In speaking to him last week, here's what he's found."

UPSELL PHRASE #19: DO YOU HAVE [FILL IN THE BLANK]? (VARIATION: WHAT TYPE OF [FILL IN THE BLANK] DO YOU HAVE?)

This is a great question to ask just as the customer is about to make a purchase or they're about to approve a proposal. I was recently at a woodworking store buying supplies. I'm at the counter and the salesperson says, "Do you have a buffer?"

I said, "No."

"Well, if you really want your project to shine, I would seriously consider getting one. Let me show you why." He then proceeded to show me 2 pieces of wood. One that used a buffer and one that didn't. "Can you see the dramatic difference?"

I said, "Yes."

He added, "The spindle is only $99. If you're going to be working on a lot of pieces, I would seriously consider getting one." He then handed me the box, which I thought was a brilliant sales move. And yes, I did buy it!

168

UPSELL PHRASE #20: "CAN YOU THINK OF ANYTHING ELSE?" (VARIATION: "IS THERE ANYTHING ELSE THAT YOU NEED?")

This is a great question to ask a client after they've exhausted their list of what they need. Recall that customers often times reach the point of decision fatigue and simply don't want to make any more decisions. What's great about this phrase is that it gives the customer a chance to take a mental pause and think to make sure there isn't anything else they may have forgotten.

"Bill, can you think of anything else?"

Bill responds, "No, I don't think so."

Here's a good opportunity to use another Upsell phrase like: "Do you have ...?" or "Something you might want to consider is ..."

This is a good list but I'm sure you can think of a few more phrases to help initiate an Upselling conversation. The above examples are meant to give you some ideas, and how you would incorporate them into your sales process.

May I suggest that you review the Upsell phrases one more time and pick 2 or 3 that you'd like to begin using in your salesprocess. Remember, use your words. Say it the way you would say it so it comes across naturally.

When it comes to using these Upsell phrases, the goal is to be genuine in your desire to help your client make a better buying decision. Review the phrases above and select at least 3 that you feel fit with your sales process and your sales style. Lastly, be intentional in applying them until they become an automatic part of your sales presentation.

UPSELLING STRATEGY #15

Mine Your Losses

I want you to put yourself in the following situation. You're selling pools*. Which means you have one shot at getting the deal. No mulligans or do-overs. If you lose the deal, you lose the deal. You qualify the client by asking relevant and pertinent questions. You ask for clarification when things are clear. You provide insight when appropriate and you listen empathetically to make sure you understand what the client wants and needs. You're methodical about your pool design and you communicate clearly with your client what the process of building a pool is and how long it will take. Your timeframe is competitive.

Up to this point you've invested 10 hours, which includes travel to the customer's location twice (i.e., first walkthrough and then the design proposal), a customized design and virtual render of all the pool with amenities so the client can visualize what they are getting, and a detailed proposal with a timeline.

The client, after a week of thinking about it, notifies you that they decided to go with someone else and they're very hesitant to share any additional information as to why they decided to choose another company. Can you relate? Now what do you do? Better yet, what can you do? Is there anything left to do?

* I like using the pool industry in my examples because it covers the sales gamut of selling: products, services, warrantees, upsells, cross-sells and it can be both a simple B2C sale to a homeowner or a complex B2B sale to a commercial or government entity.

170

Most salespeople and companies would put the client in the lost column and move on to the next. That's part of the game of sales. You win some and you lose some. But is it possible to turn a loss into a win? I didn't think so until I spoke with Ed Gibbs, President of Gib-San Pools.

Every year Ed takes his team to an off-site sales training event that lasts 3-4 days. I've had the pleasure of being part of these events. His events are unique in that it covers more than just topics on sales. I also included sessions on personal growth and development, yoga, and 6am morning medication sessions for the whole team. Yes, before a full day of training, Ed wants his salespeople to be centered and focused on why they're at the conference.

During the most recent sales training conference, which happened to be in Antigua, Guatemala, Ed and I got into a discussion about lost deals. The topic of conversation was what to do, if anything, with lost deals.

Ed mentioned the 'stack of proposals' that represented lost deals back at the office. To most, that stack would be a sore reminder of the losses the company has endured in the previous year. Not to Ed. Ed has an 'acres of diamonds' mindset when it comes to finding opportunities amongst his losses. "We may have lost the deal, but we haven't lost the client," he exclaimed.

To which I asked, "What do you mean?"

"It's all in how you look at the numbers and understanding customer Lifetime Value (LTV)," he added.

At that moment he guided me to the nearest flipchart and wrote the following:

- Time invested in proposal = 10 hours

- Proposals lost: 75

- Hours lost: 750

He continued, "If you look at how many hours have been lost, you might be discouraged, and you should be."

He then flipped the sheet and began to write the following:

- 75 Deals Lost

- Average deal size $50K

- Total Revenue lost: $3,750,000

"And, if you look at the raw numbers, gross revenue, that figure is even more depressing. This number would make anyone flinch, but that's looking at the glass half-empty."

Ed went on to explain that his profit on any new pool construction was 10%, which means that although he lost $3,750,000 his net profit lost was more like $375,000, give or take. He then gave me a quick summary of the numbers:

- 75 Deals Lost

- Average deal size $50K

- Total Revenue lost: $3,750,000

- 10% margin on construction: $375,000

"Still a significant number," I added.

Ed leaned in with a cheeky smile and said, "Yes, no doubt. But you have to look at the other side of the sales equation. There's product sales and then there's service and maintenance sales. We service pools and we can also recommend upgrades to the pool once they've been installed. And unlike construction, where we only make 10% on the service and maintenance side, we make 30%."

Ed flips to another blank sheet and begins to write the following:

- Client Life Cycle: 7 years

- Pool Service (Cleaning, Opening, Closing): $5,000 per year

- Pool Repairs: $1,000 per year

- Customer Lifetime Value: $42,000 + Pool Upgrades or Replacements: $20,000

He went on to explain that if you have a customer for 7 years, with an average service cost of $5,000 a year, minor pool repairs of $1,000 per year and during that timeframe you upgrade or replace equipment to the value of $20,000, each customer is worth $62,000.

And, if the profit margin on service and maintenance is 30%, the Customer Lifetime Value = $18,600.

He then flipped to one last blank sheet and wrote the following:

Profit from Construction $375,000/ Profit from Service $18,600 = ~20

"Victor, if I can get at least 18 of the 75 lost construction deals to buy their service and maintenance from me, that would be the same as winning those construction deals. Sometimes, you make more money on the backend than the frontend. It's all how you look at it. When you lose, remember, you can always mine your loses," Ed concluded.

This all made perfect sense and I was happy to receive this valuable lesson. But my brain immediately thought: Why would a homeowner allow a different company to service their pool? The longer I thought about it, the more it became clear that there are several reasons why they would do so:

- Many salespeople never follow up with their customers and simply move on to the next deal. If the customer has no relationship with the salesperson or the company, they are more willing to work with another company for their service and maintenance.

- Maybe the homeowner isn't happy with the level of service they're getting from the company that built their pool and may be willing to go with someone else.

- When the homeowner moves away and there's no relationship with the construction company, the new homeowners might re-evaluate their service (and cost) and decide to find a competitive bid.

The salesperson's (or company's) inability to maintain a relationship leaves a gap for a competitor to slide in. Which gets us back to managing your customer data using a smart Customer Relationship Management (CRM) system. Even though you lost the proposal, it doesn't necessarily mean you've lost the client.

FORTUNE IN THE FOLLOW-UP

Making customer follow-ups, even on lost deals, has to be built into the sales process. We've all heard the saying, "The money is in the follow-up." Too often when we lose a deal, we log into the CRM system, check the client lost, and move on to the next potential prospect. This isn't always a good move, as illustrated by the Gib-San Pool example.

Let me state the obvious. Equipment always fails. Service often lacks. Two great reasons for implementing a follow-up to not only acquired customers, but more importantly to customers you've lost. Dissatisfaction is a powerful motivator for switching.

If a client doesn't buy from you, it's worth exploring why. Have a customer service representative, not the salesperson, call the customer up directly and ask why they've decided not to buy or to go with another competitor. The objective here is not to rescue the sale, but to get a better understanding of why the customer decided to go elsewhere. This information could be valuable for future deals and should be captured in a CRM.

Lastly, it's worth mentioning that maybe the deal wasn't lost, it was simply delayed. It wasn't a good time for the homeowner to make a decision, for whatever reason. Having a follow-up process for 'status quo' deals is a must.

Here's my challenge to you, and the main message of this book: make follow-ups and Upselling a part of your sales process. Find those hidden sales opportunities that are all around you.

UPSELLING STRATEGY #16

Compensate the Upsell

This last Upsell strategy is for sales managers and leaders who want to incentivize salespeople to Upsell but don't know where to start.

Salespeople feel the pressure from three different entities in any company when it comes to increasing a company's revenue.

	Focus
Senior Level Executives	Revenue Goals
Product Managers	Profit Center
Sales Leaders	Sales Target
Salespeople	Sales Quota
Clients	Product Solution

176

1. Senior Level Pressure: Senior management is pressuring the sales team to increase the number of new clients, increase the order size, increase the close rate, or all the above. Getting new clients isn't as easy since access has become more of a challenge. Getting clients to commit or close on a deal is more complex than ever since more decision-makers are involved in the decision-making process. We are then left with increasing the average order size (i.e., Upsell them on buying more) in order to move the revenue needle. Senior executives begin to apply pressure downward.

2. Product Management Pressure: Product managers develop new products or services and are under the gun to make their business unit profitable. A lot of upfront cost (investment) goes into developing a new product for the market. Therefore, product managers need to justify the investment, as quickly as possible, with the help of salespeople. Salespeople on the other hand are so overwhelmed with selling their existing products that they don't have time to stop, understand, promote and pitch a new product, so they stick with what they know and is guaranteed. Product managers, along with senior executives, apply pressure on the sales leadership as well.

3. Sales Leader Pressure: With senior executives and product managers applying more and more pressure to sell, a sales leader has to find ways to get salespeople to move in a given direction: sell specific products, focus on new accounts, sell value not price, etc. In order for these behaviors to take hold, a leader has to convince salespeople that, in the case of Upselling, it's worth the time and effort to justify a modification in their behavior. You can show them how it will benefit the company, but that's not enough. You can show them how it will benefit them if they deploy Upselling strategies throughout the sales process. You might get some change. But in the end, compensating them is the biggest lever you have to modify their behavior.

4. Salesperson Pressure: Pressure is a funny thing. When the right amount of pressure is applied, you can get the results you want. When too much pressure is applied, the results could be disastrous or irreversible. Feeling the pressure of management all the way from the top, the salesperson has to find a way to make the number or risk losing their position or job altogether.

One of two things could happen. The salesperson either ups their game and begins to perform, or decides that the requests (demands) are unreasonable and leaves the company.

In selling we are all familiar with the concept of reactance, which is the negative reaction clients have to being pressured into making a decision. Not feeling comfortable being pressured, clients will generally pull back or hold off on making any decision. This can sometimes signal the seller, incorrectly, that they need to apply more pressure to get the deal closed.

The manager's dilemma: Not enough pressure and the salesperson might underperform or not achieve their potential. Too much pressure and the salesperson may leave or, worse, begin to pressure the client, which never ends well. Much like pressure can deform a piece of metal, so too can too much pressure deform a sales process.

Is there a better approach to aligning everyone's interest other than just applying pressure to make the number?

PRODUCT MANAGEMENT AND SALES LEADER MASH-UP

Let's begin with the basic premise that salespeople will sell the way they sell and getting them to change behaviors is a challenge. Salespeople will always take the path of least resistance.

- They will sell what they're used to selling

- They will sell it the way they're used to selling

As a past leader in sales, I understood quite clearly the challenge of getting salespeople to focus on selling other products or services not in their direct line of sight. In order to modify a behavior, you have two options:

1. Coercion: Do this or else

2. Cognitive: Explaining to them why it's important and how they can help create a win-win (i.e., company and salesperson)

Both of these approaches will work up to a point, but in the end you won't get very far continuously threatening someone, and while Upselling is a logical win-win, the resistance to sell is more at a primal, if not emotional, level.

The key to Upselling falls in the lap of product management and the sales leader. Product management has to find ways to 'sell' the sales leadership and salespeople on why they should focus on selling more of their existing or new products. Sales leaders must, in turn, find ways to give incentives to the sales team by providing the proper compensation for their perceived added effort.

A mash-up is a creative work, in the form of a song or movie, that is created by blending two or more works (i.e., pieces) to create a completely unique end product. By combining different elements, the new work retains the nostalgic modes of the old and creates an exciting new fusion.

Product management and sales leaders need to get together and create a mash-up that combines the positioning power of a new product and behavioral incentives to create a mash-Upsell environment.

MASH-UPSELL CHECKLIST

Step 1: Upsell Matrix. Let's begin with the Upsell Matrix introduced earlier. Salespeople need a road map in terms of what to Upsell, especially if their product portfolio is vast (100s of SKUs) or if new products have been developed with which they have little or no knowledge of how. Documenting those other products in a matrix is a great first step.

Product Sold	Upsell Options	Special Instructions
Product #1	Item A Item B Item C	Value Propsition: (Description) Potential Objections: (Rebuttals)
Product #2	Item D Item E Item F	Value Propsition: (Description) Potential Objections: (Rebuttals)
Product #3	Item D Item E Item F	Value Propsition: (Description) Potential Objections: (Rebuttals)

Step 2: Training Modules. If you want salespeople to sell or promote your product to existing clients, you have to train them. Training comes in both long-form and short-form. Long-form training might be a 1-2 workshop on how the product works, how it'll work for the client and how to position it. Short-form training is the new star on the training block. Creating micro-courses or micro-videos on new products is a great strategy. Production management should get marketing involved in creating small, bite-sized, snack-able content that salespeople can consume between meetings or while traveling (i.e., listen

while driving, watch while flying).

Step 3: FAQs. This step could be combined with the previous training step. Frequently Asked Questions (FAQs) are a key component of training and getting salespeople up-to-speed quicker. Create a list of gotcha questions a client might ask the salesperson along with the appropriate responses they should give. Remember, the salesperson will resist selling the latter for fear of being asked and not having the answers. Training salespeople and giving them access to short-form courses and FAQs will go a long way in reducing their nervousness about selling something new.

Step 4: SPIFFS. A SPIFF is a special incentive, usually monetary, given to a salesperson for a very specific target accomplishment. By attaching a SPIFF to a specific behavior, you are more likely to get a salesperson to focus on that behavior. If you want a salesperson to begin offering a new product to their client, you can influence their behavior to do so by 'SPIFFing' that product. Let's say you want a salesperson to begin selling product X. You can attach a monetary SPIFF (percentage, fixed number) for every product X sold. If the new product has a cost of $10,000, you can give the salesperson a 10% SPIFF or fixed bonus (e.g., 500) for every Product X sold. Here are some examples of where you can apply a SPIFF:

- Add-Ons: Any add-ons sold with an existing base product.

- Tier of Product: If you offer multiple tiers of products (e.g., T1, T2, T3), you can choose to create a SPIFF for top-level tier sales (e.g., T3).

- Number of items per first sale: Count the number of items on the first sale to a client and attach a fixed SPIFF for every added item. For example, if the first order contained 5 items, then you can give a $500 bonus ($100 per each item).

- Second Minimum Sales: A second order placed by a new client above a certain revenue level.

- Frequency: If a client submits more than X orders in a given timeframe. For example, the client submitting 6 orders in a 1-year period would warrant a SPIFF.

- Average Deal Size.

- Average Margin per Deal: To discourage heavy discounting.

SPIFFs come in all shapes and are only limited by the sales leader's creativity.

STEP 5: Review & Adjust: Care should be taken when developing a SPIFF program alongside a compensation plan. You want your salespeople to stay focused and motivated to sell their existing base products which generate the majority of your company's revenues. As you implement SPIFF programs to begin moving new (or existing) products into the market, make sure that long-term goals (customer satisfaction) are not sacrificed for short-term gain (incentive). Make sure to monitor and review your incentive program quarterly as you roll out your new SPIFF program. Every new program, no matter how well thought out, carries with it the seeds of unintended consequences. Be vigilant.

Lastly, making Upselling part of the sales process, monitoring key metrics for results and incentivizing the right behaviors is a winning combination.

APPENDIX A

Outbound vs. Inbound

Outbound marketing utilizes a PUSH approach, which pushes the product in front of a prospect using various tactics:

- Cold-Calling
- Direct Mailing from paid or rented email lists
- Pop-ups and Pop-under banners
- Banner Ads using Webpage Cookies
- TV & Radio ads
- Video Ads on websites

Outbound can be considered to be interruptive and sometimes intrusive. Today's consumers are well aware of the different tactics used by Marketing to gain their attention and, therefore, have developed attention blindness (i.e., can 't see them anymore) to cope with the hundreds of messages they encounter every day.

And while Outbound Marketing has made an effort to use technology to put the right ad in front of the right person at the right time, by its very nature it still intrudes on a person's online or offline activities.

Inbound Marketing, on the other hand, utilizes a PULL approach to attract customers, thereby reducing the intrusive factor associated with Outbound. Instead of interrupting the client, Inbound Marketing focuses on attracting the customer by providing helpful content online. If a client goes online to browse or do research, the goal of an Inbound marketer is to provide relevant content to entice potential clients to click on their content.

Inbound Marketing uses the following tactics to get in front of their prospects:

- Search Engine Optimization (SEO): When a client searches online, your company's site will appear, organically, on the first or second page of results.

- Search Engine Marketing (SEM): When a client searches online, your advertisement (ad) will appear in the results. These ads are paid for by your company.

- Blogging or Vlogging: Creating written content or videos that you post on your website.

- Newsletter Campaigns: Information sent out to those on your mailing list.

- Social Media: Create ads, videos or articles that you can share on the various social media channels.

In today's market, a combination of Inbound and Outbound is effective. Outbound Marketing can be said to be more seller-centric, where the seller is reaching out to potential clients. Inbound is more customer-centric, as it focuses on attracting potential clients by providing useful information to help clients make a better decision.

APPENDIX B

Discounting: The Easy Way Out

"If you only have a hammer in your toolbox, all the world looks like a nail. If discounting is your only tool, then all the world is a sale based on price."

Managers believe that their product offering delivers superior value to their clients, but they readily admit that they (their salespeople) have a difficult time communicating and persuading clients of their product or solution's real and applied value. Their concerns are justified.

Salespeople (account managers) more often than not choose to take the path of least resistance when it comes to selling their product or solution. The path of least resistance usually means discounting the price, as opposed to selling the value, in order to close the sale.

- Why does this happen? What's the root cause of this behavior?

- Lack of complete product or solution knowledge?

- Lack of understanding of the product's applied value?

- Lack of training on how to communicate the product's value?

• Salespeople are unable or unwilling to sell the value?

When discounting is the main tool for selling, the results are as follows: Sales go up, profitability goes down, and the company now has to sell more just to maintain margins. How? Let's consider for a moment the following profitability formula:

Profitability = Margins x Velocity

When margins are high and the frequency of the products being sold (velocity) is low, the company can still maintain high profitability. But when margins are low due to discounting, the company has to sell more, more often (velocity) if it wants to maintain its profitability.

So it follows that when a salesperson discounts products or solutions (i.e., lowers margins), it has to sell more, more often (velocity), to maintain the company's profitability at an acceptable level.

In order to increase velocity, the salesperson either has to convince existing clients to buy more (i.e., increase their buy frequency, Upselling or Cross-Selling) more often, or fill the pipeline with many new clients. Both alternatives provide their own set of challenges.

Yet, by understanding the product's value and being able to communicate the applied value to the client, salespeople can challenge the client's assertion of wanting a better discount and refocus them on the value they are receiving. The end result is less price concessions (discounts), which in turn increases profitability and minimizes the pressure on the salesperson to find new opportunities and close more sales.

It's worth highlighting here that the benefit to the salesperson who learns how to sell value is that they can reduce the number of opportunities they need to focus on (i.e., quality opportunities) and not spread themselves so thin as to dilute their sales impact in their territory as they try to find new business to make up for heavy discounting.

WHO LOSES?

When your potential client receives a competitive bid that is priced at 20-30% cheaper than your solution, how do you react? How do you help the client justify the difference? Or do you immediately offer some type of bonus or discount? Are you aware of the value differential your product offers? Or are you trained only on feature differential without understanding the real value?

For example, your company sells a technology solution that is priced at $50,000 on a per-site basis. You are bidding on a project that will require 100 sites to be developed (i.e., a $5 Million dollar opportunity). Your closest competitor has priced his solution at $40,000 per site.

The client then asks you to explain the difference in their pricing. You reply by telling the customer of the superior support and service he will receive and how you will be personally involved to make sure all goes well. The client is not convinced since your competitor has claimed the same level of service and support.

At that very moment, both you, the salesperson, and the client are unaware of your product's value. Since you couldn't quantify the real value of the price difference, you are in no position to defend your higher price. Which also means that neither you or the client are aware of the real value of what's being offered. Because you are unable to articulate the value, the client will most likely go to the value default by asking for a better price. Unable to defend your value (because you don't really understand it), you capitulate and lower the price to $40,000.

Your company just lost $1M ($10,000 discount per site multiplied by 100 sites) in revenue because you didn't know or couldn't articulate the product's real value.

Ironically, there are times when the client is well aware of the differential value and how your solution will benefit his company. The client may have already estimated that although your system is priced at $10,000 per site higher, based on their internal studies the client has found that the value of the system at each site is actually worth $60,000 in cost reductions and revenue increase in the first year alone. The client has already decided to go with the higher priced system but, knowing that you are unaware of your product's value, demands a better price. Again, you capitulate by lowering your price to $40,000 and your company loses out on $1M in revenue.

- You're happy because you closed the deal.

- The customer is happy because they were able to gain $60,000 worth of value for $40,000.

- Your manager is not happy as they have to refill a $1M gap in the forecast.

You now have to go out and find a way to sell more to your existing clients or find a new client to make up for the discount.

In either case, you pay what is often referred to as an ignorance tax. This is the amount of money you (and the company) forfeit for not knowing the product's value as it applies to each client or market segment.

It's easy to understand senior management's frustration with salespeople. Selling on price alone instead of positioning the product's value is tantamount to giving away your company's profits. The equivalent of writing a check to the client, which you hand to them with every product you deliver. Imagine a product arriving at their location with a check attached to it. That's essentially what discounting translates to.

Salespeople are trained to learn a product's features and sell the benefits, yet they're not taught to sell the overall value. A benefit is not a value element unless it can be anchored to an increase in profit or a decrease in cost to the client.

THE OTHER SIDE

Just as we train salespeople to sell value and resist discounting, company's hire purchasing or buyers with a specific mandate lower cost from all of the company's suppliers. Buyers are focused on getting the price down. Just like we send salespeople to get trained to sell at higher prices, buyers are sent to training workshops to learn how to negotiate and gain price concessions. It's easy to see why price is the centerpiece of selling in today's market.

You, the seller, are trying to get a higher price and the buyer is trying to get the lowest price. Who wins? The person that argues best for their position.

Think about it for a moment. If you don't know your value and are incapable of defending yourself when challenged on price, and you will be challenged, you will lose the argument.

Buyers, on the other hand, are trained to challenge price and not evaluate value. The latter is not their mandate. So while salespeople are putting upward pressure to move out of the basement of the commodity supply chain, buyers are putting concessionary downward pressure to convince them otherwise.

Buyers can point to price reduction to justify their position. It would be hard for a buyer to go back to their top management and explain why they're paying more based on some estimated value the company may receive. The path of least resistance presents itself again. Buyers will work hard to get price concessions vs. accept higher prices and have to justify the value to their top management.

The greatest irony in any buyer-seller relationship is that buyer's continuous demand more advantages (e.g., product features or software enhancements), but at the same time they are reluctant to pay more for the additional value they demand.

Clients are always going to ask for a discount or better pricing, that's reality. That said, while giving a client a discount in order to close a deal may seem like a good idea at the time, there are 3 major downsides, aside from the obvious impact on profit margins.

1. Devalued your product - When you discount your product, you've essentially transmitted to your client that theproduct was overpriced to begin with. Discounting devalues your product in the client's eyes.

2. Conditioned the Buyer: By conceding a discount, you areconditioning the buyer to ask for discounts in the futurewhen you attempt to sell them something else.

3. Suspicion: When you gave the client a better price via adiscount, the client may be left wondering why you didn'tgive them that price in the first place. Were you trying togouge them? From that moment forward the client willbe suspicious of any claim regarding 'bottom line' pricing in future proposals.

While discounting may seem like an easier route to closing than pushing back and positioning value, in the long run you'll damage your long-term position and relationship with the client.

APPENDIX C

Client Conversations

We've all had that moment when we finished delivering a flawless presentation where every question was answered and every concern addressed, yet the client needed more time to think about it or kicked the can down the road (i.e., let's revisit this next quarter or next year). You leave the meeting with a mental blend of frustration, confusion and a tinge of anger. Or, worse, you leave the meeting questioning your own ability to sell and position your product's value and you carry that doubt onto your next meeting.

To understand why the majority of clients won't make a buying decision, you have to begin by first analyzing your current presentation. In that presentation, are you dealing with the customer's stated needs, but more importantly, are you also addressing the client's unstated or unconsidered needs?

- **Stated Need:** The client tells you exactly what they're looking for.

- **Unstated Needs:** The client doesn't mention specific needs because they feel vulnerable in disclosing their real needs. The client's trust level is very low.

- **Unconsidered Needs:** The client doesn't mention specific needs because they haven't considered those needs in the first place. The client doesn't know enough to ask the right questions.

A good example might be a client, let's say a technology company, who is looking for a better solution to their current Client Relationship Management (CRM) system. The client will tell you (i.e., Stated Needs) what they specifically find wanting in their current system.

In considering whether or not to move forward with your CRM solution, the client is thinking about how much time and effort it's going to take to implement this in his company and the adoption rate of the new solution. Because these matters seem more like internal issues, the client never raises these concerns (i.e., Unstated Needs) during the meeting. The client is then left thinking as you wrap up your presentation: (a) How much time, money and effort is this going to take to switchover? (b) How long will the training be and how will that impact deliverables? (c) Will they use this new system?

Clients are also hesitant to pull the trigger on new projects if the change does not create enough separation from the existing solution. Creating separation is more than just a differentiation or comparison matrix of features, it's about providing the client with a new way of looking at an old problem (i.e., unconsidered needs).

For example, let's say that this CRM system comes with a pre-recorded voicemail option that allows their salespeople to leave a pre-recorded message if the call goes to voicemail. While the CRM system is leaving a message, the auto-dialer is already calling the next prospect. Having pre-recorded messages allows the salesperson to record various messages to leave depending on which stage of the prospecting process he's in. Pre-recorded messages deliver consistency in both the quality of the message and the content that has been approved by the company.

This is a feature that a client will find interesting and they can see how it could be used to help salespeople make more calls.

During the presentation, you demonstrate the feature. Then, your next move should be towards quantifying the value of that feature. You say,

"John, every voicemail left by the CRM saves the salesperson anywhere from 30 - 60 seconds per call. This may not seem like much but if we assume 1 minute per voicemail and the daily call rate is 100, that's 100 minutes saved per day. Multiply that by 22 working days in a month and that's 2,200 minutes per month, which is equivalent to 37 hours per month, or almost a week's worth of calls. Add to this that the amount of time salespeople spend on actual sales activity is around 40% per day, this CRM pre-recorded option is a much-needed efficiency booster."

At this point, the client is now looking beyond the feature (i.e., pre-recorded voicemails) and sees how this new CRM could help him solve a bigger problem they're having: level of sales activity per salesperson.

A good visual for addressing these 3 needs, Stated, Unstated and Unconsidered, is the analogy of an iceberg. If we accept that with every iceberg, on average, 10% is visible above the surface of the water and 90% lies below, then you should model your presentation, either for a first-time sale or an Upsell, with the iceberg visual in mind.

Too often salespeople focus their time and energy during a presentation to address the 10% (Stated Needs) that they believe will interest the customer. They focus on the new features, the bright lights, the cool options, and so forth. Let's consider this a **Level 1** presentation where the features and benefits are covered exhaustively. These types of presentations usually lead to a price conversation, since competitors are espousing similar claims.

A Level 2 presentation goes below the client's chilled or cool disposition to uncover deeper issues that might prevent the client from moving forward. As stated in the CRM example, these issues could be conversations around time, effort and the adoption of a new solution.

This Level 2 conversation focuses on assuaging the client's deep-seated concerns about change. Selling is about change and clients have to be sold on the 'Why', but more importantly on the 'How' it will make their lives easier, more efficient and more profitable. Simply put, the client wants to know if it's worth the time, money and effort to change. While they may not come out and say so plainly, nonetheless that's what they're thinking. And that's the conversation you need to have with the client; a heart-to-heart talk about their daily concerns.

The deepest conversations, and by that I mean the most impactful, occurs at **Level 3: Unconsidered Needs**. At this level you are looking to move beyond comparison and assuaging fear and aim at shifting their way of thinking or their way of viewing your solution. These types of conversations require a real deep understanding of your product, the client's business and the client's competitive market space.

A good way of getting to know your client's business and market forces at work is to consider Michael Porter's Five Forces Model. Michael Porter, researcher and economist at the Harvard Business School, challenges the notion of selling against your competitor (us vs. them mindset) by asking us to take into consideration the client's point-of-view (POV).

- **Force 1:** Your clients are competing with existing rivals towin business in the market. (Competition)

- **Force 2:** Your clients must anticipate new entrants whowill enter the market. (New Rivals)

- **Force 3:** Your clients compete with competitors who offera substitute solution to their products. (Substitute Products)

- **Force 4:** Your client must also deal with buyers who arealways looking for a better deal in terms of quality andprice. (Price Pressure)

- **Force 5:** Your clients must also contend with supplierswho want to raise their price while lowering the valuethey deliver so they can be more profitable. (SupplierPressure)

These 5 forces determine your client's profitability structure and the challenges they face in trying to grow their revenues. Understanding these 5 forces, in the context of how it affects a client's buying decision or motivation, will enable a salesperson to have Level 3 conversations where you now move into the trusted advisor position and are viewed as an enabling resource not just another vendor.

To do so, here's a presentation process or exercise you should do before visiting your next client.

Step 1: List 5-7 stated needs or wants you know the client will want to know about or discuss. For example, that the new

CRM system has new features to make the client's life easier.

Step 2: List 3-5 unstated needs where you put yourself in the client's shoes and think through what internal changes or challenges (e.g., time, effort, adoption, etc.,) the client will have to consider if they buy your solution.

Step 3: List 1-3 unconsidered needs. These are viewpoints that your clients have not considered. Again, this requires that you go deep in both trying to understand the client's business space and how your solution can provide unintended and unconsidered benefits. For example, how much time pre-recorded voicemails can improve efficiency and reduce Cost of Sales (COS).

Step 4: Create a presentation or pitch that covers each of those types of needs.

Step 5: After each presentation, reflect on how it was received and make the necessary adjustments to the script (what was said) and the sequence (when it was said) until you feel that you're consistently moving into Level 2 and/or 3 conversations.

For every new or Upsell opportunity, create an Iceberg model. In any Upsell situation, the sale should be that much easier if the customer experience has been good.

Upselling at this point is less of a challenge since the major hurdle of trust and execution are not in question. The emphasis is more on justification of buying rather than credibility.

ADDITIONAL RESOURCES

Visit VictorAntonio.com for Keynote and Workshops

SalesVelocityAcademy.com for Online Training